SPECIAL TIME EDITI

Harry Pot

Inside the Tale That Enchanted the World

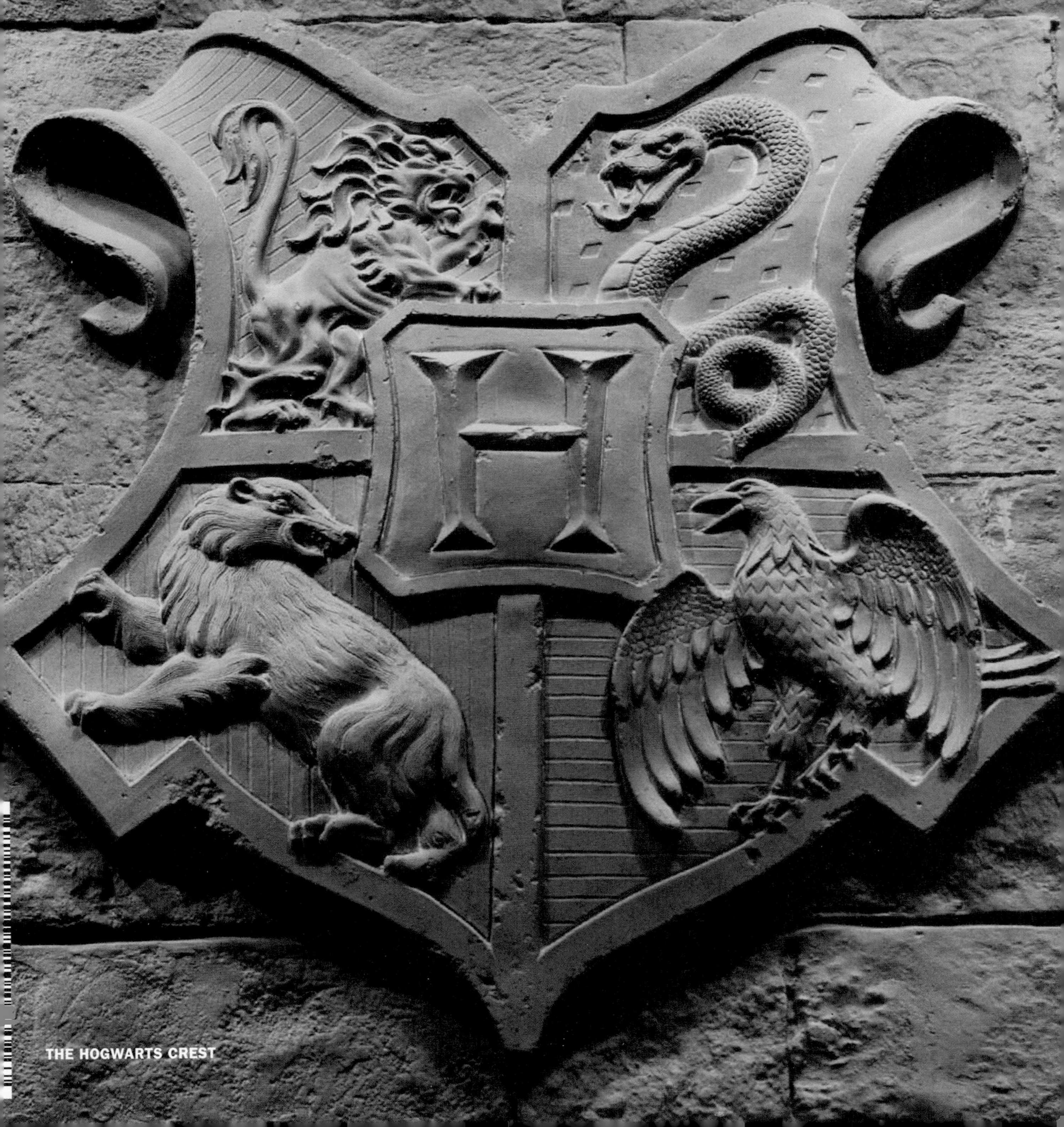

THE HOGWARTS CREST

Contents

Parts of this edition were previously published by TIME.

The film cast at Hogwarts, 2007

INTRODUCTION

The World's Most Beloved Wizard Turns 20

BY SARAH BEGLEY

IN THE SUMMER OF 1997, TONY BLAIR WAS SETTLING IN AS THE U.K.'S new prime minister, Bill Clinton was working to pass the Balanced Budget Act, Timothy McVeigh was convicted of the Oklahoma City bombing, the Pathfinder probe landed on Mars, Gianni Versace was murdered in Miami Beach, and Puff Daddy's "I'll Be Missing You" knocked Hanson's "MMMBop" off the No. 1 spot on *Billboard*. It was also the summer when the world met Harry Potter.

Early reviews of J.K. Rowling's series rightly compared her to the masters of fantasy writing. Like C.S. Lewis and J.R.R. Tolkien, she took inspiration from a wide range of sources: Christian theology, folklore, Greek and Shakespearean tragedy, Arthurian legend, Dickensian plotting and 20th-century history (especially the rise and fall of Hitler) all shaped the story of the Boy Who Lived. Yet these factors combined to create a work so original and iconic that it's easy to see its influence on an entire generation of successors and imitators.

For all her cerebral elements, Rowling was also a master of the mundane. What makes for a quirky shop? A cozy pub? A thrilling sports match? Her whimsical answers to these questions played as big a role in making Harry Potter a cultural behemoth as did her interrogations of morality. As many critics and enthusiasts have noted, part of the genius of the books is that because Harry has been raised in total ignorance of the wizarding world, he discovers its structures and vagaries right alongside the reader. Like our own world, it is full of variation, tempting readers to ask themselves how they'd fit in. Children who read the books wonder what house they'd be placed in if they attended Hogwarts, what kind of wand they'd have, what their Patronus would be.

Yet as personal as the series feels—and to the most devout fans, it's very personal indeed—it ultimately succeeds because the story is universal. Harry's path closely follows Joseph Campbell's concept of the Hero's Journey, from the call to adventure to the triumph over death. It's the arc found in works from the Bible to *Star Wars*.

Harry's tale is further rooted in practical questions of what it means to be a good person in the contemporary world. Rowling emphasizes that family is paramount: Harry's bond with his de-

SPELLBOUND Harry and Co. charmed the globe.

ceased parents, particularly his mother, is vital. But she concedes that family can also be the pits, as the dreadful Dursleys prove. She celebrates Hermione's diligence as a student but also acknowledges that book smarts won't take you very far without friendship and courage. She preaches the necessity of resisting evil. And she shows that goodness is not a state of mind but a choice, made again and again, to do the right thing. The Harry Potter series has become almost like a bible for readers who treat its lessons as morality plays. "We've all got both light and dark inside us," as Sirius Black tells his godson. "What matters is the part we choose to act on."

Twenty years later, the world looks very different from that first summer with Harry. Strictly in terms of Potter books, the series has been over for a decade. Though the 2016 publication of the script to the play *Harry Potter and the Cursed Child* was celebrated with midnight release parties reminiscent of the original series's publication, this time many readers opted to stay home and hit "download" on their e-readers—which were only just beginning to be available when the final book, *Harry Potter and the Deathly Hallows*, came out in 2007.

But some things haven't changed. As the first generation of young Harry fans has grown up and begun to have children of their own, a new crop of readers ages into the series, dreaming of enchanted dinners in the Great Hall and evenings spent in the Gryffindor common room. New wizarding stories will continue to arrive on the Pottermore website and in the form of four more *Fantastic Beasts and Where to Find Them* movies that are due in the coming years.

For decades or even centuries to come, children will begin their encounter with the first sentence that was printed 20 years ago: "Mr. and Mrs. Dursley, of number four, Privet Drive, were proud to say that they were perfectly normal, thank you very much." Thank goodness nothing else about Harry Potter is.

The Timeline of Potter

Looking back on 20 years of the wizard who conquered the world

June 26, 1997

***Harry Potter and the Philosopher's Stone* is published in England in an edition of 500 copies.**

Dec. 27, 1998

Harry's first appearance on the *New York Times* best-seller list.

Sept. 4, 1999

The first known Harry Potter fan-fiction story, "Harry Potter and the Man of Unknown," is posted to FanFiction.net.

July 2000

The *New York Times* creates a children's best-seller list after the first three Potter books spend a year atop the adult-fiction list. (Taking over the adult No. 1 spot after Potter moves to the kids' section: Danielle Steel's *The House on Hope Street*.)

8.3 million

July 21, 2007

Number of copies *Deathly Hallows* sells in the U.S. during its first 24 hours on sale

July 2007

By the time the final book, *Harry Potter and the Deathly Hallows*, is released, publisher Bloomsbury has spent some £10 million (nearly $20 million) on an army of guards, satellite tracking systems and legal contracts to prevent any leaks.

July 11, 2007

U.S. premiere of *Order of the Phoenix*, in which Harry and Cho Chang share a kiss.

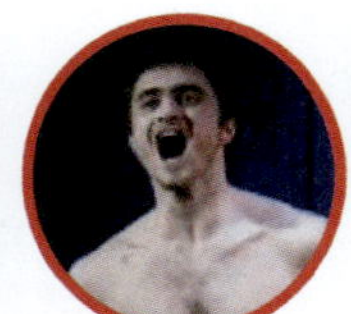

Feb. 27, 2007

A revival of *Equus* premieres in London, starring 17-year-old Radcliffe in a role that includes a nude sex scene.

June 18, 2008

Sales of Harry Potter books pass the 400 million mark. (They still trail the Bible and Mao's Little Red Book.)

July 29, 2008

IBM demonstrates software that scans, sorts and stores personal memories, named Pensieve, for Dumbledore's basin of thoughts.

July 15, 2009

Quidditch costumes get a makeover—with added protective gear reminiscent of classic American-football padding—in *Harry Potter and the Half-Blood Prince*.

August 2010

Warner Bros. files suit against Swiss manufacturer Magic X for its line of Harry Popper condoms.

Jan. 6, 2011

Universal's Wizarding World of Harry Potter in Orlando announces the sale of its millionth (nonalcoholic) Butterbeer.

July 15, 2011

Deathly Hallows 2 is released in the U.S.

July 8, 2011

"No story lives unless someone wants to listen—so thank you, all of you."

—**ROWLING,** to fans at the London premiere of *Harry Potter and the Deathly Hallows: Part 2*

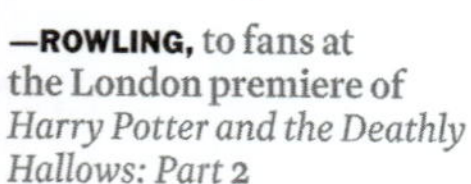

July 8, 2000

The fourth Harry Potter book, *Goblet of Fire*, reaches stores. The next in the series, *Order of the Phoenix*, won't appear until 2003; fans refer to this dark period as the three-year summer.

Nov. 4, 2001

Harry Potter and the Sorcerer's Stone, the first movie in the series, premieres in London.

Emma Watson, Rupert Grint and Daniel Radcliffe at the very first press conference

Nov. 6, 2001

The Simpsons pays its first homage to Harry, in the Halloween special "Treehouse of Horror XII," in which Bart and Lisa enroll at Springwart's School of Magicry, attracting the attention of the villainous Lord Montymort and his snake flunky, Slithers.

June 22, 2002

The brothers of the band Harry and the Potters play their first show (in their parents' backyard in Massachusetts), kicking off wizard rock, the indie-rock movement inspired by J.K. Rowling's books.

July 22, 2002

"I loathe Harry Potter. Those books are hopeless and massively clichéd—bad thinking and bad writing. And they will vanish. In spite of all the hype and all the 120 million copies, they're bound for the rubbish heap in five, six years."

—Literary critic **HAROLD BLOOM** in an interview with TIME

Oct. 25, 2002

Richard Harris, who played Hogwarts headmaster Albus Dumbledore in the first two movies, dies of Hodgkin's lymphoma at age 72. He is replaced by Michael Gambon.

November 2002

Rowling files suit against the publishers of *Tanya Grotter and the Magical Double Bass*, a Russian Harry Potter knockoff. The Tanya Grotter books go on to sell nearly 3 million copies, though Rowling's court victory blocks them from most Western markets.

March 7, 2003

Two years before he becomes pope, Joseph Ratzinger writes that the Potter books . . .

"are subtle seductions, which act unnoticed and, by this, deeply distort Christianity in the soul before it can grow properly."

May 2004

Tokyo University professor Susumu Tachi demonstrates a prototype invisibility cloak at a conference in San Francisco. It works by projecting objects behind the wearer on the front of the cloak, creating the illusion that you can see through it.

July 2005

In Vancouver, 14 copies of *Harry Potter and the Half-Blood Prince* are accidentally sold before the official release, prompting a court order forbidding the buyers to disclose any of its contents before its on-sale date.

July 31, 2011

Limited registration begins for the fan site Pottermore, where Rowling releases new content about the Harry Potter universe.

July 27, 2012

Rowling reads from *Peter Pan* at the opening ceremony of the London Olympics.

Sept. 27, 2012

Rowling publishes *The Casual Vacancy*, a social satire.

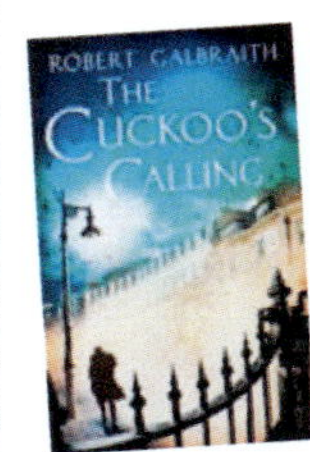

April 4, 2013

Rowling publishes a crime novel, *The Cuckoo's Calling*, under the pseudonym Robert Galbraith. It receives positive reviews but sells only 1,500 copies in the U.K. before the true authorship is revealed three months later. It goes on to top best-seller lists.

Feb. 15, 2015

A TV adaptation of *The Casual Vacancy*, starring Dumbledore actor Michael Gambon, airs in the U.K.

July 30, 2016

Harry Potter and the Cursed Child opens in London, with a script by Jack Thorne and based on a story by J.K. Rowling, Thorne and director John Tiffany.

Nov. 10, 2016

Fantastic Beasts and Where to Find Them opens in theaters.

April 9, 2017

In its ninth month in London's West End, *Harry Potter and the Cursed Child* wins a record-setting nine Olivier awards, including Best New Play.

By Lev Grossman and Allie Townsend

POTTERMANIA From its viral beginnings, the love for Harry and his tale spilled over.

CHAPTER ONE

Phenom Meets Frenzy

ON A DAY TRIP TO NEW YORK CITY AT AGE 8, I STOPPED into a bookstore with my parents. Another little girl—whom I'd never met but who didn't let that stop her—came up to me and pressed a copy of *Harry Potter and the Sorcerer's Stone* into my hands. "Want a recommendation?" she asked. "You have to read this."

Variations of this scene played out around the world in the late 1990s, as millions of kids became acquainted with Harry Potter. The series found instant adoration among kids and parents, bookworms and reluctant readers alike.

By the summer of 1999, word-of-mouth recommendations were moot: everyone had already heard about the boy wizard with the lightning-bolt scar, and they lined up in droves to purchase *Harry Potter and the Prisoner of Azkaban*, which came out two months later in the U.S. than in the U.K. If you were very lucky, as I was, you had a family friend in England to mail you a copy before your friends had it.

Sometime after I had finished the third book, my mother asked me why I hadn't picked up a new novel yet. "Nothing compares" was my melancholic response.

—Sarah Begley

Game Change

The exploits of a young wizard brought a new kind of magic to children's literature

BY PAUL GRAY

FOR THE UNINITIATED, HERE ARE THREE SUREfire, clinically tested signs that you are a Muggle: (1) You spot a boy or girl whose forehead is emblazoned with a paste-on tattoo in the shape of a purple lightning bolt and have no idea what you are seeing. (2) You still believe reading is a lost art, especially among the young, and that books have been rendered obsolete in our electronic, hot-wired age. (3) You don't know what a Muggle is.

Fortunately, such ignorance has become almost ridiculously easy to remedy. Simply place yourself in the vicinity of a child, just about any child anywhere, and say the magic words "Harry Potter." If, for instance, you utter this charm to Anna Hinkley, 9, a third-grader in Santa Monica, Calif., here is what you will learn: "What happens in the first book, Harry discovers that he's a wizard, and he's going to a school called Hogwarts School of Witchcraft and Wizardry. At the station he meets a boy named Ron, who's also going to Hogwarts. And on the train, they meet a girl named Hermione..." Given enough time, Anna will tell you the entire plot of the 309-page *Harry Potter and the Sorcerer's Stone*, which she has read, she confides, "seven or eight times."

That book, of course, is only the opening chapter of a story that has become one of the most bizarre and surreal in the annals of publishing. The whole Harry Potter hubbub seems practically outlandish: the still-proliferating pages that fans post almost daily on the Web, the word-of-mouth testimonials from parents marveling that their nonreading children (even boys!) are tearing through the Potter books and begging for more, the confessions of a growing number of adults not so young that they find these young-adult books irresistible. What on earth is going on here?

If there were an easy answer, nearly every other writer on earth would by now be beavering away at imitations of J.K. Rowling's formula for success, and the world would be teeming with best sellers about prepubescent wizards attending bizarre boarding schools somewhere in the north of Britain. And, in fact, it is not particularly hard to figure out the rules governing the Harry Potter books. Place appealing characters in interesting yet perilous situations and leave the outcome in doubt for as long as possible. Nothing new here, nothing that storytellers as far back as Homer did not grasp and gainfully employ. But, as devoted Harry Potter fans have learned, knowing a magic charm is not the same thing as performing magic. Rowling's secret is as simple and mysterious as her uncanny ability to nourish the human hunger for enchantment: she knows how to feed the desire not just to hear or read a story but to live it as well.

That is why so many people both young and naive, and older and jaded, have surrendered to the illusions set forth in Harry Potter's fictional world. They want to believe the unbelievable, and Rowling makes it easy and great good fun for them to do so. How pleasant to be persuaded that an orphan named Harry Potter who has lived for 10 years with the Dursleys (his cruel aunt and uncle and their hateful son, Dudley) in a faceless English suburb—specifically 4 Privet Drive, Little Whinging—learns shortly after his 11th birthday that he is really a wizard. What's more, he is famous throughout the wizard world: although his parents were murdered by the evil Lord Voldemort (so feared that he is referred to only as "He-Who-Must-Not-Be-Named"), the infant Harry survived the attack with a lightning-bolt-shaped scar on his forehead.

Every event in the Potter books follows seamlessly from his initial self-discovery. Harry may be a skinny kid with glasses, green eyes and an unruly shock of black hair, but he also harbors uncertain potentialities. Did he thwart Voldemort's assault because of innate goodness or because he carries, even as an infant, a strain of evil more powerful than that of the Dark Wizard? This question will remind some of the *Star Wars* films and the tangled destinies of Darth Vader and Luke Skywalker. But once such comparisons begin, they can lead in many directions.

Harry's shuttling between two worlds is also reminiscent of Lewis Carroll's Alice, L. Frank Baum's Dorothy in her journey to Oz, and the time-traveling earth children who keep reappearing in C.S. Lewis's seven-volume *The Chronicles of Narnia*. Like them, Harry is young enough both to adapt to altered realities and to observe them with a minimum of preconceptions. Also, the sorcerer's stone in the first Harry Potter book bears an obvious kinship with the all-powerful ring pursued in J.R.R. Tolkien's *Lord of the Rings* trilogy.

But Rowling's indebtedness to classical fantasy literature should not overshadow the liberties she takes with the form. Most notably, her wizard world is not at all remote from daily realities. It takes a cyclone to transport Dorothy to Oz. In contrast, Harry can walk a few steps through a London pub near Charing Cross Road and enter Diagon Alley, a wizard shopping bazaar, where he and his classmates meet late each summer to buy school supplies. And getting from there to Hogwarts is a snap—Harry and his friends go to King's Cross Station and board the Hogwarts Express.

When they arrive, the crenellated towers of Hogwarts look just the same as they did last year. Why not? The school is more than 1,000 years old. Such unchanging details make Rowling's innovations in each book seem particularly dramatic. In the third book, *The Prisoner of Azkaban*, a sympathetic professor tells Harry why dementors merit fear: "They breed in the darkest, filthiest places, they create decay and despair, they drain peace, hope and happiness out of any human who comes too close to them . . . Even Muggles feel their presence, though they can't see them. Get too near a dementor and every good feeling, every happy memory will be sucked out of you. You'll be left with nothing but the worst experiences of your life."

The speech in Azkaban is one of the darkest and most unsettling in the Potter books. It creates a vivid physical embodiment of a painful mental state, which Muggles call depression, and it demonstrates Rowling's considerable emotional range. She can be both genuinely scary and consistently funny, adept at both broad slapstick and allusive puns and wordplay. She appeals to the peanut gallery with such items as Bertie Bott's Every Flavor Beans, a wizard candy that means what it says on its package: it offers every flavor, ranging from chocolate and peppermint to liver and tripe and earwax. But Rowling also names the Hogwarts caretaker Argus Filch, evidently hoping that a few adult readers will

Harry Potter by the Numbers

COPIES SOLD WORLDWIDE
450 million

EDITIONS IN TRANSLATION
79

ESTIMATED VALUE OF FRANCHISE
$25 billion

AMOUNT MOVIES HAVE GROSSED WORLDWIDE
$7.7 billion

The Places

The geography of the wizard world is closely interwoven with regular, everyday locations. Wizards—and readers—can easily move back and forth, but most ordinary folks don't know how, so here's some help

Hogwarts: School of Witchcraft and Wizardry. Housed in a castle more than 1,000 years old, it offers seven years of rigorous, if unorthodox, education to a handpicked elite of potential sorcerers

Hagrid's Cottage: Home of the school's gruff but lovable gamekeeper

The Forbidden Forest: The dark woods surrounding the Hogwarts grounds

Hogsmeade: An all-wizard village near the school where students after their second year are allowed to visit. Attractions include the Shrieking Shack, "the most haunted dwelling in Britain"

Diagon Alley: A street of shops selling wands, cauldrons, broomsticks, robes and other magic paraphernalia

Gringotts: The central wizard bank, with vaults far below the streets of London, operated by Goblins (*not pictured*)

Platform Nine and Three-Quarters: The track at King's Cross Station where students gather each fall to board the *Hogwarts Express*

The Home of the Dursleys: 4 Privet Drive, Little Whinging, the scene of Harry's unhappy childhood

IN THE BEGINNING "Harry Potter strolled into my head fully formed," says author J.K. Rowling.

remember that Argus, in Greek mythology, was a watchman with eyes all over his body. And even if no one else picks up the reference, it's the sort of touch that can prompt an author's inward smile.

Rowling says the urge to be a writer came to her early, during what she describes as a "dreamy" childhood inner life. She began writing stories when she was 6. She also read widely, whipping through Ian Fleming at age 9. Sometime later, she discovered Jane Austen, whom Rowling calls "my favorite author ever." She was writing a novel for adults when, during a 1990 train ride, "Harry Potter strolled into my head fully formed."

Rowling insists that she never consciously set out to write for children but that working on Harry Potter taught her how easily she could tap into her childhood memories. "I really can, with no difficulty at all, think myself back to 11 years old [Harry's age when the series opens]. You're very powerless, and kids have this whole underworld that to adults is always going to be impenetrable." That's a good description of the social setup she portrays at Hogwarts, where the students have stretches of time with little or no adult supervision. Rowling believes young people enjoy reading about peers who have real control over their destiny. "Harry has to make his choices. He has limited access to really caring adults."

She can be both genuinely scary and consistently funny, adept at both broad slapstick and allusive puns and wordplay.

One of the interesting things about Hogwarts in the Potter books is that it contains no technology at all. Light is provided by torches and heat by massive fireplaces. Who needs electricity when you have plenty of wizards and magic wands? Who, for that matter, requires mail pickup and delivery when a squadron of trained owls flies messages to and from the school? Technology is for Muggles, who rely on contraptions because they cannot imagine the conveniences of magic. Who wouldn't choose a wizard's life?

The Still-Expanding Potterverse

How *Fantastic Beasts* and *Cursed Child* have evolved from the rest of Harry's magical world

By Ashley Ross

Original Potter books and movies

Fantastic Beasts and Where to Find Them
BOOK, MARCH 2001
MOVIE, NOV. 2016

Harry Potter and the Cursed Child
OPENED JULY 2016

SETTING

1990s England, mostly at Hogwarts School of Witchcraft and Wizardry

1920s New York, mostly at the Magical Congress of the USA (America's wizard HQ)

Modern-day England, mostly at Hogwarts and the Ministry of Magic (the U.K.'s wizard HQ)

HEROES

Harry, Ron, Hermione, Dumbledore—and many, many more

"Magizoologist" Newt Scamander, wizard sisters Queenie and Porpentina "Tina" Goldstein, and magicless Jacob Kowalski

Albus Severus, Harry's youngest son

VILLAINS

Voldemort and the Death Eaters

The titular beasts, who run amok after escaping Newt's bewitched briefcase

Debatable—but some signs point to Harry, since his legacy causes problems for his son

INSPIRATION

Rowling's childhood and complicated relationship with her father

A "real" Hogwarts textbook, written by Rowling and released in 2001

An original short story by Rowling, Jack Thorne and John Tiffany

ACTORS

Daniel Radcliffe, Emma Watson and Rupert Grint, among others

Eddie Redmayne, Katherine Waterston and Colin Farrell, among others

Jamie Parker as Harry, Paul Thornley as Ron, and many others

LINGO

Muggle (the U.K. term for a nonwizard), *Butterbeer* (a sugary drink) and *Wingardium Leviosa* (the spell for levitation)

No-Maj (the U.S. term for people who can't perform magic)

Augurey, a dark bird whose cry foreshadows rain—and possibly death. It is the symbol of Delphi, Voldemort's daughter

CENTRAL HOUSE

Gryffindor, known for bravery, nerve and chivalry

Hufflepuff, the Hogwarts house known for patience and loyalty

Slytherin, known for cunning and ambition

The Group Who Shall Not Be Named

One of the most intense Harry Potter fan followings gathers in New York

BY ALEXANDRA GENOVA

IT'S 9 P.M. IN CENTRAL PARK, AND A CLOUD OF cloaked figures huddle beneath the glowing moon. Photographer Amy Lombard thought she was lost, but as two women donning witch hats hurry past to join the crowd, she knows she's in the right place.

For The Group Who Shall Not Be Named (TGW), the world of Harry Potter is not consigned to the pages of a novel or cinema screen. As the largest Potter fan association in the world, its 2,000 New York–area members are testament to the power of J.K. Rowling's magic. "Our group is here to spread the love of Harry Potter and the associated love of literature and reading," organizer Jonathon Rosenthal says. "The world is a pretty tough place, and there's a lot of things that push you down ... I believe there's nothing wrong with having a little bit of magical fun, even as an adult." And just as Rowling makes no secret of her continued absorption in Potterworld—the final book in the original series by no means spelled the end—her fans also remain as devoted as ever.

Lombard, for her part, has spent time documenting the New York group as part of a wider project studying the world of online communities that meet offline. But the dedication and commitment of this group's members stand out as something special. "Jonathon runs this so consistently," Lombard tells TIME. "Some groups don't meet that often. But you see the same people coming to this meet-up and new faces as well." TGW holds a monthly meet-up as well as special events to satisfy any number of tastes, including Wizard Rock Shows, Harry Potter–themed crafting and in-costume ice-skating.

The testimonials from members are impressive. One enthusiastic attendee, known as Deanna the Elder, found three Potter books lying on a downtown Manhattan sidewalk back in 2001. Having never read any Potter, she took the books home, devoured them, and they "basically changed [her] life." At a time when 9/11 was a very recent memory, Deanna found that the books offered her emotional refuge from a world in a state of flux. For many, TGW provides the same. "I have had people literally tell me that they are staying in New York because of the people they met through the meet-up," Rosenthal says. "I admit the city is hard to live in. It's challenging. But I love being able to provide something that connects people to the city and gives them something they wouldn't have anywhere else."

The extraordinary popularity of Rowling's books has flowered a vast Potter-head network. But for TGW members, a shared love of all things wizard is just the starting point. The meet-ups create a milieu of openness and positive energy, a magical atmosphere where great friendships and

ALL THE WIZARDS The group, comprising 2,000 members, has been photographed by *Vogue*.

even marriages have been forged. What may begin as a discussion about chapters and characters will quickly widen into other literature and interests. "First-time convention-goers are always shocked because they'll go into an elevator at an event, full of people they don't know, and they will instantly start having conversations," says Rosenthal. "And that doesn't happen anywhere else. It's incredibly rare."

Parading in New York in costume is a popular activity for the group, and Lombard is not the first to see the aesthetic potential. As self-confessed "photo hams," TGW members are willing subjects, and the group has had scores of professional photo shoots, including one for *Vogue* magazine. As for the general public, they almost never get a negative response. "Most people are really, really thrilled to see us," says Rosenthal. "You get the whole range of reactions, starting from the little kids whose jaws drop, teenagers who are kind of goofy about it and then adults who are like, 'Oh, my God, I love what you're doing. I wish I could do this.' And we are like, 'You can! Here's our card.' "

With members ranging from 18 to 80 years old, the group's attraction clearly cuts through typical social barriers. "Just the fact that this group of people can approach life in this way and still have this love is something that is magical, literally," says Lombard. As a wise wizard once said: "Of course it is happening inside your head, Harry, but why on earth should that mean it is not real?"

Where Dreams Come Alive

The Wizarding World of Harry Potter lets ordinary Muggles step into J.K. Rowling's universe

BY RICHARD CORLISS

ONE REASON SO MANY WIZARDS WANTED TO GET rid of Albus Dumbledore was that he was soft on Muggles. Now he's gone too far: the headmaster has let those decidedly unmagical humans into Hogwarts. Tens of thousands a day swarm through a 20-acre swatch of Universal's Islands of Adventure theme park in Orlando, Fla. Beneath the looming redoubt of Hogwarts School, these undocumented aliens clog the quaint main street of Hogsmeade, buying Sneakoscopes and Fanged Flyers at Zonko's Joke Shop, mailing postcards (with special Potter stamps) from the Owlery, posing for a photo in front of the Hogwarts Express, slurping Butterbeer at the Three Broomsticks restaurant. Why, the clerk of the Hogsmeade branch of Ollivander's is bestowing holly wands on Muggle children. The whole spectacle is enough to turn a pureblood's stomach. Somebody alert the Ministry of Magic! Page Lucius Malfoy! This may require the attention of ... You-Know-Who.

The visitors are all votaries of J.K. Rowling's seven Potter novels, which have sold hundreds of millions of copies worldwide, and the movies the books have spawned, which have earned billions in theaters and quillions more on DVD and streaming. In April 2016, Universal Studios opened London-themed Potter attractions, uniting the two areas by a four-minute train ride and one name: the Wizarding World of Harry Potter. Universal spent hundreds of millions to concoct a grand, obsessively accurate replica of Rowling's vision. The author made sure of that. Rowling had final approval on all aspects of the Wizarding World,

ADVENTURELAND Hogwarts Castle, opened in 2010, is part of the Potter-themed area spanning two Universal parks.

which opened in 2010. From her home in Scotland, Rowling signed off on the design, rides and some 600 pieces of merchandise, most of them unique to the park. Her involvement helped induce many of the films' stars—including Daniel Radcliffe (Harry), Emma Watson (Hermione) and Rupert Grint (Ron)—and artists (designers Stuart Craig and Alan Gilmore) to work with Universal's park sorcerers, Mark Woodbury and Thierry Coup. Rowling may hope to transform Muggles into wizards. Universal's goal has been to turn the Potter legions' ardor into a major magnet for the company's two Florida theme parks and three hotels.

The great age of theme-park creation in the Sunshine State spanned a decade, from Disney-MGM Studios in 1989 to Islands of Adventure in 1999, with Universal Studios Florida and Animal Kingdom in between. The four parks, along with Disney's existing Magic Kingdom and Epcot, consolidated the Orlando area's status as a top vacation destination. This millennium has seen less expansion: a new attraction here (Universal Studios' The Simpsons, the funniest, best-scripted ride ever), a fireworks display there (the entrancing Wishes at

TRAIN OF THOUGHT Above: The Hogwarts Express steams in place at Universal's Islands of Adventure. Opposite, from top: A coaster ride on twin tracks sends two speeding trains into orbit, within 18 inches of each other. The small gift shops draw queues of fans.

the Magic Kingdom). The Great Recession took a big bite out of family-vacation budgets—attendance at Universal's Florida parks dropped about 10% in 2009—and stifled the ambition to build. Even the Wizarding World is simply new sections of an existing park.

WORLD OF WONDER

But what's here is choice. Unlike the candy-colored palette of Disney parks, black, gray and white are the dominant shades at the Wizarding World: the daunting slate of Hogwarts, the subtly ornamented shops, all capped by the rooftops' perpetual snow, which in the oppressive summer heat serves as both a daydream and a taunt to sweltering guests. Cute, or Disney's robust American form of it, is out. Quaint British style is in. The Wizarding World is a bit like Stratford-upon-Avon, except that Rowling, not Shakespeare, is the presiding genius. And you don't walk into the house she once lived in; you experience the dream she created.

Parks need rides, and the Wizarding World has three—two borrowed from the Lost Continent, a part of Islands of Adventure that Universal foreclosed on to make room for Harry. One is the Dragon Challenge, formerly Dueling Dragons. It's been adapted into a race from the Triwizard Tournament in *Harry Potter and the Goblet of Fire*, with the tracks renamed Hungarian Horntail and Chinese Fireball and the preshow area decorated with the Goblet, the Triwizard Cup and other Potter totems. The Flight of the Hippogriff (previously the Flying Unicorn) is a more sedate ride showcasing one of Hagrid's favorite magical creatures. At one point, an animatronic hippogriff bows to you. Bow back.

The big attraction is Harry Potter and the Forbidden Journey, which blends the scenic vistas of Disney's wondrous Soarin' ride with the jolting narrative adventure of Universal's Spider-Man. Strapped into your broomstick pod, you are led by Harry, Ron and Hermione on a forbidden journey (remember, you're a Muggle) skyward out of Hogwarts, observing a Quidditch match, eluding the grasp of a cranky Whomping Willow and practically

getting heatstroke from a fire-spuming dragon. It's an impressive, harrowing, high-octane trek—not for the little ones.

But take them anyway so they can enjoy the splendid preshow. (They stay in a waiting room while you're on the ride.) As the line snakes through the "Gryffindor common room," wizards in wall frames chat cattily about you; a holographic Dumbledore—the great Michael Gambon—explains the school rules; and Harry, Ron and Hermione appear to invite you on the journey. Post-ride, you exit through Filch's Emporium of Confiscated Goods, which sells many of the books' gadgets, from Death Eater masks to the coveted Golden Snitch. Then stop for a meal at the Three Broomsticks, with traditional English food like fish-and-chips and Cornish pasties (of high quality for a theme-park eatery) and the Hogsmeade-exclusive Butterbeer—basically cream soda with a secret foam topping, and delicious.

No question, the Wizarding World is a hit. That's clear from all the blogs grousing about the hours visitors can spend waiting to get on a ride or even to be admitted into Potterland. Some of the shops are so small that people often must line up

outside just to buy stuff. (Guests staying at Universal hotels get into the park an hour before the official opening. Or you can just wait for an off-peak month in the fall.)

But even if you don't have time for the Forbidden Journey, you can get the full Potter experience just walking around, admiring the evocative precision of the decor, immersing yourself in Hogsmeade. Here, as at Disney, the park is the ride. And the Wizarding World is one fabulous trip.

CHAPTER TWO

The Woman Behind the Wizard

J.K. Rowling, one of history's all-time best-selling authors, reflects on the spell she cast

BY NANCY GIBBS

WHEN THE FINAL BATTLE WAS OVER AND THE LAST SECRETS of the seven-book, 17-year journey were spilled, Jo Rowling did what grieving, grateful and emotionally exhausted people do: she ransacked the minibar.

She'd known from the start that Harry Potter would survive his ordeal; the question was how she would handle her own. She had been holed up on deadline in the Balmoral Hotel in Edinburgh, Scotland, to escape the bedlam at home, writing the climactic chapter in which her hero walks into the dark forest to give his life for those he loves. And though she knew that all would be well in the end, "I really was walking him to his death, because I was about to finish writing about him," she says. It's her favorite chapter in her favorite book—but when she finished, "I just burst into tears and couldn't stop crying. I opened up the minibar and drank down one of those pathetic little bottles of champagne."

Rowling calls her time with Harry "one of the longest relationships of my adult life," her rock through bereavement, a turbulent marriage and divorce, single motherhood, changes of country, fear of failure—and transcendent joy, on the day

WHERE IT ALL BEGAN Above: Edinburgh's Elephant House café is where Rowling started writing the Potter books. Right: Rowling with the young actors who would become her franchise's megastars.

a wise man at Bloomsbury offered her $2,250 and agreed to print 1,000 books. Fast-forward through the life of Harry. In 2007 *Harry Potter and the Deathly Hallows*, the seventh and final book in the series, sold 15 million copies worldwide in the first 24 hours it was on sale, breaking the record that had been set successively by each of the previous three books. (To put that in perspective, Book Six, 2005's *Half-Blood Prince*, moved more copies in its first day—9 million—than *The Da Vinci Code* did in its first year.) Meanwhile, the movie version of Book Five, *Order of the Phoenix*, made $645 million, and plans for the Orlando, Fla., theme park were unveiled. *Forbes* magazine put Rowling second only to Oprah as the richest woman in entertainment, and as the first person to become a billionaire by writing books.

The writer's journey that began in 1990 ended in 2007, leaving Rowling a little more margin to savor ballet recitals and grocery shopping and intensive, often ingenious charitable work. A woman of high energy and a short fuse, she looked almost serene when we met for this piece, nearly a year after she'd finished the last book in the series. She was dressed in black with a long, gray belted sweater, dark red nails and a funky black ring the size of a walnut. But as we sat and talked over coffee, you could hear the longing when the conversation shifted back to Hogwarts, as though we'd retreated to a safe place but couldn't stay there long. "I can only say, and many of my more militant fans will find this almost impossible to believe," she says, "but I don't think anyone has mourned more than I have. It's left the most enormous gaping hole in my life."

She's funny and self-mocking and earnest by turns but always unguarded and unrehearsed, especially since now, after all this time, she can talk about the things she had to keep secret because her readers did not want their pleasure spoiled by knowing how things would turn out. "It's a massive, massive sense of release," she says, to be able to answer any question, tell the backstory with obsessive fans who want to know the middle names of characters down to the third generation. She doesn't actually need to talk to Barbara Walters, because her fans know where to find her: her website, which includes news, a diary, a rubbish bin for addressing the more idiotic rumors, and answers to both the frequently and the never asked questions.

It's not just Harry's secrets that can now be revealed. It is Rowling's as well. The biggest mystery, appropriately, had to do with Rowling's own soul. As soon as her tales achieved fame, they were denounced by fundamentalist clerics from the U.S. to Russia to the Muslim world. The pope warned about their "subtle seductions" that might "distort Christianity in the soul." One day when Rowling was shopping for toys in New York, a man recognized her. "He says, 'I'm praying for you,' in tones that were more appropriate to saying, 'Burn in hell,' " she says, "and I didn't like that 'cause I was with my kids. It was unnerving. If ever I expected to come face to face with an angry Christian fundamentalist, it wasn't in FAO Schwarz."

Through it all, Rowling didn't really fight back. Talk too much about her faith, she feared, and it would become clear who would live and who would die and who might actually do both. After six books with no mention of God or Scripture, in the last book Harry discovers on his parents' graves a Bible verse that, Rowling says, is the theme for the entire series. It's a passage from I Corinthians in which Paul discusses Jesus's resurrection: "The last enemy that shall be destroyed is death."

"Many people may feel that they own Harry. But he's a very real character to me, and no one's thought about him more."

It turns out that Rowling, like her hero, is a Seeker. She talks about having a great religious curiosity, going back to childhood. "No one in my family was a believer. But I was very drawn to faith, even while doubting," she says. "I certainly had this need for something I wasn't getting at home, so I was the one who went out looking for religion." As a girl, she would go to church by herself. She

TICK TOCK The Balmoral Hotel in Edinburgh is where Rowling holed up to finish the final book in the series.

still attends regularly, and her children were all christened. Her Christian defenders always thought her faith shined through her stories. One called the books the "greatest evangelistic opportunity the church has ever missed." But Rowling notes that there was always another side to the holy war. "At least as much as they've been attacked from a theological point of view," she says, the books "have been lauded and taken into pulpit, and most interesting and satisfying for me, it's been by several different faiths." The values in the books, she observes, are by no means exclusively Christian, and she is wary of appearing to promote one faith over another rather than inviting people to explore and struggle with the hard questions.

Rowling's religious agenda is very clear: she does not have one. "I did not set out to convert anyone to Christianity. I wasn't trying to do what C.S. Lewis did. It is perfectly possible to live a very moral life without a belief in God, and I think it's perfectly possible to live a life peppered with ill-doing and believe in God." And now she climbs into a pulpit of her own, and you can tell how much this all matters to her, if it weren't already clear from her 4,100-page treatise on tolerance. "I'm opposed to fundamentalism in any form," she says. "And that includes in my own religion."

She has certainly found her disciples. Critics can dismiss Rowling's grownup fans as "kidults," but especially as the series unfolded, her audience expanded far beyond children and her impact well beyond entertainment. In addition to some 300 wizard-rock bands, reams of fan fiction and countless websites, the books have inspired outfits like the Harry Potter Alliance, an online group co-founded in his late 20s by Andrew Slack, a consultant in Boston, around the rallying cry "The weapon we have is love." When *Deathly Hallows* was released, the group organized house parties from Australia to South America and coast to coast in the U.S. to raise awareness of genocide in Darfur, in a kind of "What Would Harry Do?" campaign. "We can be like Dumbledore's army, who woke the world up to Voldemort's return, and wake our ministries and our world to ending the genocide in Darfur," Slack urged Harry Potter Alliance members in tones of earnest camaraderie.

When asked about the group, Rowling practically levitates off the couch, spilling her coffee along the way. "It's incredible, it's humbling, and it's uplifting to see people going out there and doing that in the name of your character," she says. She's especially pleased by the group's choice of mission, and the old Amnesty International worker in her surfaces. "What did my books preach against throughout? Bigotry, violence, struggles for power, no matter what. All of these things are happening in Darfur. So they really couldn't have chosen a better cause."

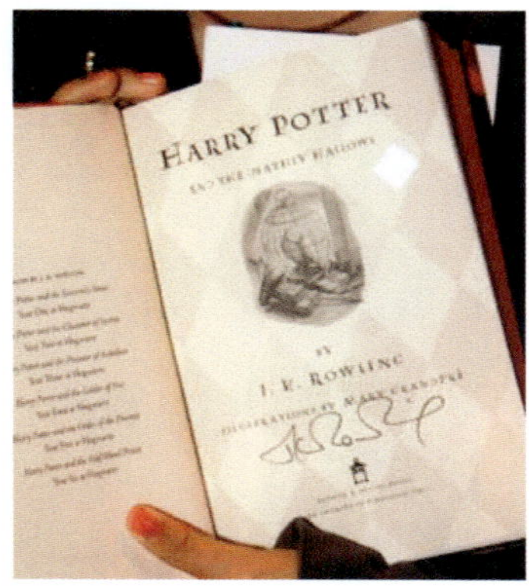

COLLECTOR'S ITEMS The chair, top, where Rowling wrote the series sold at auction for almost $400,000; bottom, a *Deathly Hallows* copy that Rowling signed for a young fan

But it's also one more example of how she will never really be in control of Harry again. She knows he's bigger than she is now and not always in ways she likes. Parents may need to let go of their children, but artists want eternal ownership, and you can feel her ambivalence at the prospect of legions of writers who want to take up Harry's story as their own. One declared at the previous summer's biggest Potterfest that, since Rowling had left the sandbox, it was open for all to play in. But this is no game to her. She can tell you exactly which character she was sketching on New Year's Eve 1990 at the moment her mother died. (It was Professor Sprout, McGonagall's "pragmatic foil," she says. "I was six months in, and I was finalizing the composition of the head table.") Knowing where you were when you first read Harry Potter, she says, is not the same as knowing where you were when you created him. If you can solve the puzzles and break the codes on her website, you can see her earliest drawings and edited manuscript pages and glimpse just how deep her devotion goes. "He's still mine," she says. "Many people may feel that they own him. But he's a very real character to me, and no one's thought about him more than I have."

He is also a billion-dollar media property and a global cultural figure. Now translated into 79 languages, the books have joined a canon that stretches from *Cinderella* to *Star Wars*, giving people a way to discuss culture and commerce, politics and values. Princeton English professor William Gleason compares the series's influence to the frenzy that surrounded *Uncle Tom's Cabin* before the Civil War. "That book penetrated all levels of society," he says. "It's remarkable how similar the two moments are." And he does not see this as a passing fad or some triumph of clever marketing. "They've spoken profoundly to enough readers that they will be read and reread by children and by adults for a long time," he says. Feminist scholars write papers on Hermione's road to self-determination. Law professors cite Dobby's tale to teach contract law and civil rights. University of Tennessee law professor Benjamin Barton published "Harry Potter and the Half-Crazed Bureaucracy," in the *Michigan Law Review*, which examined Rowling's view of the legitimacy of government. His conclusion? "Rowling may do more for libertarianism than anyone since John Stuart Mill."

And that is on top of the impact, even her critics acknowledge, of inspiring a generation of obsessive readers unafraid of fat books and complex plots. "They're easy to underestimate because of what I call the three Deathly Hallows for academics," says James Thomas, a professor of English at Pepperdine University. "They couldn't possibly be good because they're too recent, they're too popular, and they're too juvenile." But he argues that the books do more than entertain. "They've made millions of kids smarter, more sensitive, certainly more literate, and probably more ethical and aware of hypocrisy and lust for power. They've made children better adults, I think. I don't know of any books that have worked that kind of magic on so many millions of readers in so short a time in the history of publications."

IT WAS THE END OF A LONG JANUARY DAY WHEN the last page of the last chapter was complete. Rowling had finished putting on the page numbers and found herself alone in her suite at the Balmoral, feeling, she recalls, some "end-of-epic euphoria." So she danced around the room a bit and then, in a fit of creative destruction, took out her pen and wrote on the base of the bust of Hermes that stood in the window alcove, "J.K. Rowling finished writing *Harry Potter and the Deathly Hallows* in this room (552) on 11th Jan 2007."

The ending, naturally, was the most controversial part of the book. It would have been so much neater just to kill Harry. "I've known that all along," she says, but that was never her plan. To her, the most noble thing, the real bravery, is to rebuild after a trauma. Some fans were disappointed that after all his adventures, Harry's greatest concern in the end is whether his son will fit in at Hogwarts.

"It's a bittersweet ending," she says. "But that's perfect, because that is what happens to our heroes. We're human. I kept arguing that 'love is the most important force, love is the most important force.' So I wanted to show him loving. Sometimes it's dramatic: it means you lay down your life. But sometimes it means making sure someone's trunk is packed and hoping they'll be OK at school."

"No one in my family was a believer. But I was very drawn to faith, even while doubting. I certainly had this need for something I wasn't getting at home."

Rowling has only to look to George Lucas to appreciate that the pressure to return to Hogwarts will be ferocious—and some of that pressure is self-inflicted. "There have been times since finishing, weak moments," she said, "when I've said, 'Yeah, all right,' to the eighth novel." But she is convinced that she's doing the right thing to take some time."If, and it's a big if, I ever write an eighth book about the [wizarding] world, I doubt that Harry would be the central character," she says. "I feel like I've already told his story. But these are big ifs. Let's give it 10 years and see how we feel then."

It's a pretty safe bet how her audience will feel. But we'll just have to wait and prepare to be surprised.

10 Questions for J.K. Rowling

1. Why doesn't Fred appear in the woods at the end as well?

"Do you know what? I never even thought of Fred coming back. That's how I always planned it, from when the first book was finished, that the three marauders and his mother would come back. There were four heroes, as it were, in the previous generation and one of them betrayed the others, and then there were the three. So I wanted Harry to be surrounded by his mother and James and Sirius and Lupin, all of whom had died in a way for him. You know Lupin had laid down his life in Harry's battle. He didn't have to come back; he didn't have to fight. James had died trying to protect the family. Sirius very obviously had died fighting along with Harry, and then his mum, who most explicitly had died for him. I never thought of bringing Fred back at all. It was all the previous generation, and they were all strongly parental figures for Harry."

2. Did Harry die?

Rowling wrote this very carefully so that it could be read two ways. "Did he just go into a state of unconsciousness in which his subconscious tells him everything he needs to know? Dumbledore doesn't tell him anything he couldn't have figured out with some educated guesses." But in her mind, Harry entered a limbo between life and death and faced a choice about which way to go.

She explains on her website that this encounter involves some very deep laws of magic that Voldemort himself did not understand: "Having taken Harry's blood into himself, Voldemort is keeping alive Lily's protective power over Harry—except that the power of Lily's sacrifice is a positive force that not only continues to tether Harry to life but gives Voldemort himself one last chance . . . Voldemort has unwittingly put a few drops of goodness back inside himself; if he had repented, he could have been healed more deeply than anyone would have supposed. But of course, he refused to feel remorse." Also, since Voldemort is using the Elder wand, which actually belongs to Harry, neither the Cruciatus nor the killing curse work properly. "The Avada Kedavra curse, however, is so powerful that it does hurt Harry and also succeeds in killing the

part of him that is not truly him, in other words, the fragment of Voldemort's own soul that is still clinging to his. The curse also disables Harry severely enough that he could have succumbed to death if he had chosen that path."

3. What was that creature in the corner at King's Cross? (This question surprises her.)

"Harry's impulse, to the point of utter wrongheadedness, is to save. His deepest nature is to try and save, even when he's wrong to do so, when he's led into traps—'I've got to save, I've got to try to protect'—because he's been left with this very demanding legacy of his mother's that she sacrificed herself for him, and now he goes off and tries to save as many people as he can."

But this encounter with Voldemort is different. "For the first time ever, he approaches this vulnerable, naked, mutilated creature and he wants to help, but he feels repulsed for the first time ever by suffering. And he's right to feel that. This is something that has deliberately self-mutilated, as it were, that's the last maimed fragment of Voldemort's soul. I have to explain because so many have asked."

4. What was Dumbledore's wand made of? (The question she was scared she'd get.)

"That would have been quite a telling question. Because I had this elder thing in my mind, 'cause elder has this association in folklore: it's the death tree. I thought, 'What am I going to say?'" It would have given away too big a clue. But no one asked.

5. What did Dumbledore really see in the Mirror of Erised?

His family, alive and whole and reconciled.

6. Where do wizard children go to school before Hogwarts?

Most are homeschooled, because they aren't really able to control their powers, so it would be too dangerous to let them out and about.

7. Are Harry and Voldemort related?

Yes, distantly, through the Peverells; but nearly all wizarding families are related if you go back far enough.

8. Who does Draco Malfoy marry?

Astoria Greengrass, younger sister of the Greengrass family. We meet Daphne Greengrass, part of Pansy Parkinson's Slytherin posse, in Book Five when Hermione takes her O.W.L.s. Neville marries Hannah Abbott, who becomes the owner of the Leaky Cauldron. "I do have it all worked out in my mind because I couldn't stop myself doing that."

9. Where do the main characters work as adults?

Harry and Hermione are at the Ministry: he ends up leading the Auror department. Ron helps George at the joke shop and does very well. Ginny becomes a professional Quidditch player and then sportswriter for the *Daily Prophet*.

10. Was Teddy Lupin a werewolf?

No, he was a Metamorphmagus, like Tonks (who, incidentally, was a Hufflepuff).

A Good Scare

The author explains what kids need to know about the dark side

BY J.K. ROWLING

TIME *asked Rowling, whose favorite holiday is Halloween, what she thinks children should know about good and evil, magic and mayhem. This is what she told us:*

I CONSCIOUSLY WANTED THE FIRST BOOK TO BE fairly gentle—Harry is very protected when he enters the world. From the publication of *Sorcerer's Stone*, I've had parents saying to me, "My 6-year-old loves it," and I've always had qualms about saying, "Oh, that's great," because I've always known what's coming. So I have never said these are books for very young children.

If you're choosing to write about evil, you really do have a moral obligation to show what that means. So you know what happened at the end of Book Four. I do think it's shocking, but it had to be. It is not a gratuitous act on my part. We really are talking about someone who is incredibly power-hungry. Racist, really. And what do those kinds of people do? They treat human life so lightly. I wanted to be accurate in that sense. My editor was shocked by the way the character was killed, which was very dismissive. That was entirely deliberate. That is how people die in those situations. It was just like, You're in my way and you're going to die. It's the first time I cried during the writing of a book, because I didn't want to kill him. It was the cruel-artist part of me who just knows that's how it has to happen for the story. The cruel artist is stronger than the warm, fuzzy person.

My daughter has read all the books now, and I said to her about the ending of *Goblet of Fire*, "When you reach Chapter 30, Mommy's going to read it to you, all right?" Because I thought, I'm going to have to hug her, and I've got to explain the stuff. And when the character did die, I looked at her to see if she was OK, and she went, "Oh, it's not Harry." She didn't give a damn. I was almost thinking, Is this not scary at all? She was just like, "Harry's OK, I'm OK." She's a feisty little thing. In some ways, I think younger children tend to be more resilient. It's kids who are slightly older who really get the scariness of it. Possibly because they have come across more intense stuff in their own lives.

Is evil attractive? Yes, I think that's very true. Harry has seen the kind of people who are grouped

FEAR FACTOR Daniel Radcliffe has said that Ralph Fiennes's Voldemort "genuinely scared me."

I don't think there's any subject matter that can't be explored in literature. Any subject matter at all. I really hate censorship.

around this very evil character. I think we'd all acknowledge that the bully in the playground is attractive. Because if you can be his friend, you are safe. This is just a pattern. Weaker people, I feel, want that reflected glory. I'm trying to explore that.

It's great to hear feedback from the kids. Mostly they are really worried about Ron. As if I'm going to kill Harry's best friend. What I find interesting is only once has anyone said to me, "Don't kill Hermione," and that was after a reading when I said no one's ever worried about her. Another kid said, "Yeah, well, she's bound to get through OK." They see her as someone who is not vulnerable, but I see her as someone who does have quite a lot of vulnerability in her personality. Hermione is me, near enough. A caricature of me when I was younger. I wasn't that clever. But I was that annoying on occasion. Girls are very tolerant of her because she is not an uncommon female type—the little girl who feels plain and hugely compensates by working very hard and wanting to get everything just so.

I do have a real problem with gratuitous violence. Video games would be the area that most alarms me. That's one thing that I'm not too keen to have wandering into my house without me really knowing what's going on. My daughter doesn't have a PlayStation at the moment. She is desperate for one. Particularly with younger children, I don't like the idea that they're going to be blowing people up, these little humanoids on the screen, with no thought of what this really means. And doing that for points. I think there is a vast difference between that and seeing a character you care about dying in a book, experiencing those emotions, working through things that we all have to face at some point.

I don't think there's any subject matter that can't be explored in literature. Any subject matter at all. I really hate censorship. People have the right to decide what they want their children to read, but in my opinion they do not have the right to tell other people's children what they should read.

One really great thing with my parents: nothing was off-limits in my house. My mother was a huge reader, and I was allowed to read anything I wanted. There was never a sense that something might be a little too scary.

J.K. Rowling's Big Secret

How a forensic linguist confirmed the author's undercover storytelling with clues from Harry Potter

BY LILY ROTHMAN

IT SOUNDS LIKE SOMETHING OUT OF, WELL, A detective novel: the U.K.'s *Sunday Times* broke the news on July 14, 2013, that Robert Galbraith, the "first time" writer behind the critically acclaimed crime novel *The Cuckoo's Calling*, was, in fact, the nom de plume of Harry Potter creator J.K. Rowling. Galbraith was described as a former military police investigator with a surprising knack for language—that is, before "he" was unmasked as the megafamous author, who told the *Times* that writing under a fake name was "liberating."

A writer for the British paper received an anonymous tip via Twitter, in which a now deleted user claimed that Rowling was the real author of *The Cuckoo's Calling*. (Is it possible that the anonymous user was the book's publisher? As the *New York Times* noted, there's no way to rule it out.) *Sunday Times* editor Richard Brooks eventually confronted the publisher, but not before he investigated the similarities between Galbraith and Rowling.

One person involved in that process was Patrick Juola, a professor of computer science at Duquesne University, who was called in by the *Sunday Times* to analyze *Cuckoo*'s text.

"The idea of looking at people's language to know who they are goes back to the Book of Judges," Juola says, referring to the history of the word "shibboleth," the pronunciation of which was used to identify an enemy tribe in the biblical story of the Ephraimites. For his part, Juola has been researching the subject—now called forensic linguistics, with a focus on authorship attribution—for a decade and a half. He uses a computer program to analyze and compare word usage in different texts, with the goal of determining whether they were written by the same person. The science is more frequently applied in legal cases, such as with wills of questionable origin, but it works with literature too. (Another school of forensic linguistics puts an emphasis on impressions and style, but Juola says he's always worried that people using that approach will just find whatever they're looking for.)

But couldn't an author trying to disguise herself just use different words? It's not so easy, Juola explains. Word length is something the author might think to change—sure, some people are more prone to "utilize sesquipedalian lexical items," he jokes—but that can change with their audiences. What the author won't think to change are the short words, the articles and prepositions. Juola asked me where a fork goes relative to a plate; I answered "on the left," but another person might say "to the left" or "on the left side."

As one part of his work, Juola uses a program—Java Graphical Authorship Attribution Program, which is a free download available for anyone to play around with—to pull out the hundred most frequent words across an author's vocabulary. This step eliminates rare words, character names and plot points, leaving him with words like "of" and "but," ranked by usage. Those words might seem

WHAT'S IN A NAME
Rowling has written four Cormoran Strike novels (or so we think . . .).

inconsequential, but they leave an authorial fingerprint on any work.

“It doesn't prove that [the *Cuckoo* author] was Rowling, but it's a starting point,” says Juola. “In this particular case, I wasn't that certain at all.” That's because Juola was provided with relatively few texts to compare against *The Cuckoo's Calling*: Rowling's *The Casual Vacancy*, Ruth Rendell's *The St. Zita Society*, P.D. James's *The Private Patient* and Val McDermid's *The Wire in the Blood*. Of those four, *Cuckoo* showed the highest similarity to Rowling's work, but that only means the author was more likely to be Rowling than to be one of three other writers.

“It's like DNA,” Juola says. “If I find your DNA at the scene of a crime, I may be able to say that the chances are billions to one that it couldn't have been any other random person—but that doesn't prove it was you.”

And, though the beginnings of forensic linguistics may be ancient, Juola says this kind of sleuthing may be on the rise. The advent and proliferation of e-books means that almost any book can now be quickly analyzed. Rowling got only a few months of anonymity, but even that period of secrecy may not long be possible for an author of her fame. That may be too bad for authors looking for the liberation brought by a pseudonym, but anonymity has its price as well. After the *Sunday Times* unmasked Robert Galbraith as Rowling, Amazon reported an increase of more than 500,000% in sales for *The Cuckoo's Calling*.

“The idea of looking at people's language to know who they are goes back to the Book of Judges.”

FAN-TASTIC A young German reader cracks open a newly translated *Half-Blood Prince* at midnight on Oct. 1, 2005.

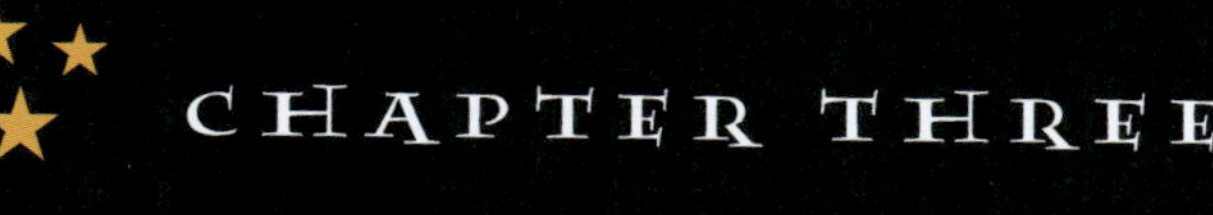

CHAPTER THREE

The Story Unfolds

PART OF THE GENIUS OF THE HARRY POTTER BOOKS IS their boarding-school framework. Spells, beasts and potions, triumphs and tragedies are fitted into the structure of daily classes and extracurricular events: the train ride back to school, the big Quidditch matches, the Yule Ball, exams. The conceit makes the story highly relatable to kids, for whom each new year begins in September, not January, but it also provides scaffolding that supports the drama and helps plot twists play out in organic ways.

Almost from the beginning, children have found the world of the books so appealing, so evocative of adventure and mystery, they begin dreaming of the day their own Hogwarts acceptance letters will arrive. They imagine taking their own school-supply shopping trips to Diagon Alley. Each successive book brings new surprises—and each is longer, darker and more suited to advanced readers. But the stories never fail to bring back the fan-pleasing professors, studies, resident ghosts, dormitory pets, excursions to Hogsmeade, meals in the great hall and inter-house rivalries that readers crave. At a school like Hogwarts, who would ever want to graduate? —*Sarah Begley*

The Whole Tale, Spell by Spell

From Quidditch scores to dark-arts secrets, an overview of each book in the series. Warning: Spoilers ahead!

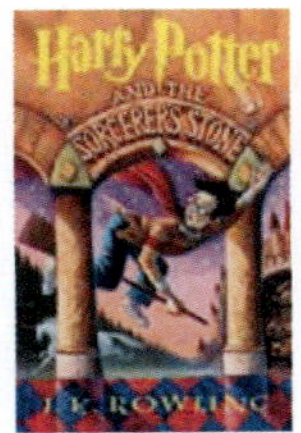

Harry Potter and the Sorcerer's Stone

THE PROBLEM: Harry's archnemesis, Voldemort, is seeking the Sorcerer's Stone, a magical artifact that could make him immortal. Harry has to find it first—and get his homework done too

QUIDDITCH UPDATE! Harry makes his house team to play the broom-bound sport of wizards

SCARY MONSTER: Fluffy, a giant three-headed dog who guards the way to the stone

MAGICAL GADGET: The Mirror of Erised. Whoever gazes into it sees what he or she desires most in the whole world

DEFENSE AGAINST THE DARK ARTS TEACHER: A position at Hogwarts with an extremely high turnover rate. This year it's Professor Quirrell, a meek, inoffensive man with a stutter—and a surprising dark side

NEW SPELL: Wingardium Leviosa. Your basic first-year levitation charm

NUMBER OF PAGES: 320

WHAT HARRY LEARNS: That wonderful, magical things lurk just beneath the ordinary

THE REVIEW: Aside, perhaps, from that lightning-bolt-shaped scar on his forehead, Harry Potter will seem familiar to anyone who has ever read a decent fairy tale. Harry, 11, is an orphan who lives with his dreadful aunt and uncle, Petunia and Vernon Dursley, and their son, Dudley. Happily, our hero receives a letter via owl informing him that he is, in fact, a famous wizard and has won a place at the prestigious Hogwarts School of Witchcraft and Wizardry. And with that, the reader and Harry together are plopped down into a world every bit as fantabulous and vividly original as those created by C.S. Lewis, Roald Dahl or, for that matter, George Lucas.

Harry Potter and the Chamber of Secrets

THE PROBLEM: Hogwarts students are being turned to stone. No one knows why or by whom, but Harry is the prime suspect

QUIDDITCH UPDATE! Harry breaks his arm in a match but wins anyway

SCARY MONSTER: The Whomping Willow, the Mike Tyson of the plant kingdom

MAGICAL GADGET: The Remembrall, a glass marble that turns red whenever its bearer is forgetting something

DEFENSE AGAINST THE DARK ARTS TEACHER: Gilderoy Lockhart, a pompous, preening, headline-hogging, egotistical idiot

NEW SPELL: Tarantallegra. Causes uncontrollable dancing in its victims

NUMBER OF PAGES: 352

WHAT HARRY LEARNS: As Hogwarts headmaster Albus Dumbledore puts it, "It is our choices, Harry, that show what we truly are, far more than our abilities."

BIRDS OF A FEATHER
Hedwig, Harry's owl, was much more than a pet—she was a confidante and friend.

GO, CAR, GO When Ron and Harry miss the Hogwarts Express in Book Two, they find alternative transit.

THE REVIEW: After the climax of *Sorcerer's Stone*, we knew Harry would be helped along in his missions by a close circle of friends and protectors. But it's in *Chamber of Secrets* that we really learn to what extent it will take a village to support Harry, as he finds himself aided by unexpected allies again and again. This sense of community will only grow in vitality as the series continues.

We also learn that while an element of destiny will always mark Harry's life, his past need not determine his future. See Dumbledore's iconic advice above. Harry may be the Chosen One, but his choices matter. With messages like these, Rowling begins to raise the stakes and add heft to the series.

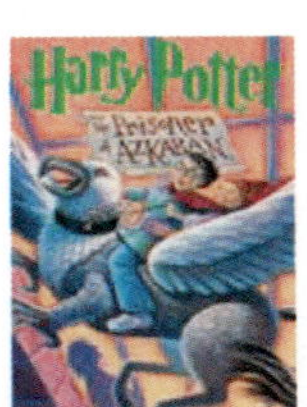

Harry Potter and the Prisoner of Azkaban

THE PROBLEM: An archcriminal named Sirius Black has escaped from Azkaban, a high-security jail for wizards, and he's looking for Harry

QUIDDITCH UPDATE! Harry gets a Firebolt, the sweeping edge of high-performance flying brooms

SCARY MONSTER: Dementors, spectral prison guards that drain the hope and happiness out of everyone around them

MAGICAL GADGET: The Sneakoscope, a gyroscopic doohickey that spins and glows when untrustworthy people are nearby

DEFENSE AGAINST THE DARK ARTS TEACHER: Remus Lupin, a sympathetic and skillful wizard with a magic—er, tragic—flaw

NEW SPELL: The Patronus charm. It creates a silver spirit that dispels dementors

NUMBER OF PAGES: 448

WHAT HARRY LEARNS: That those we have lost are always with us, in particular when we need them the most

THE REVIEW: This is where the series begins its transition onto a darker plane—and where Rowling's imagination goes from inventive to truly innovative. Rowling introduces many of the most significant and beloved elements of the series in this volume, like the Marauder's Map and the Time-Turner. It's also where she brings in some of the most significant threats: the Dementors, yes, but also the more vague sense of danger in not knowing who can be trusted. Harry undergoes one of his most emotional transitions in this novel, beginning with a great fear of Sirius and ending with true devotion. It's no surprise that many fans count *Azkaban* as the best installment in the series.

Harry Potter and the Goblet of Fire

THE PROBLEM: Signs and portents suggest that Voldemort is marshaling his forces. And Harry must face his first school dance

QUIDDITCH UPDATE! Harry attends the Quidditch World Cup (Ireland wins)

SCARY MONSTER: The Hungarian Horntail, a particularly nasty breed of dragon

MAGICAL GADGET: Portkeys, everyday objects that instantly teleport wizards who touch them

DEFENSE AGAINST THE DARK ARTS TEACHER: Alastor "Mad-Eye" Moody—scarred, wooden-legged and generally scary-looking. But his secret identity is even scarier …

NEW SPELL: The Imperius Curse. Basically, magical mind control. Few people can resist its power, but Harry is one of them

NUMBER OF PAGES: 752

WHAT HARRY LEARNS: Doing the right thing usually means doing the hardest thing. Plus, girls are complicated

THE REVIEW: Those millions who were enchanted by the first three books will almost certainly feel the same way about *Goblet of Fire*. Like its predecessors, the new novel is heavily dependent on surprises and suspense. Although *Goblet of Fire* sags a little now and then, Rowling's astonishing inventiveness in describing new wizardly wonders and her sly sense of humor usually keep things moving along briskly. Nearly every page offers something intriguing or funny. There are, for example, the odd books on magic that the studious Hermione consults, including *Men Who Love Dragons Too Much* and *Where There's a Wand, There's a Way*. No wonder the parents who started reading these books to their children found themselves hooked. But this time, some of those parents may want to keep the book away from their younger ones. The rumors that *Goblet of Fire* is darker and more violent than the first three turn out to be true.

Harry Potter and the Order of the Phoenix

THE PROBLEM: The wizarding world is divided between those who believe Voldemort has returned and those who don't, but Harry knows the threat is very real. Plus, he faces his first standardized test

QUIDDITCH UPDATE! Ron joins Harry on the Gryffindor Quidditch team

SCARY MONSTER: Thestrals: skeletal, winged horses that are gentle but creepy. They can be seen only by those who have witnessed death

BEAK LINK Harry befriends Hagrid's Hippogriff.

EYES HAVE IT Brendan Gleeson as Alastor Moody

SCHOOL'S OUT Students celebrate a distraction from their Ordinary Wizarding Level (O.W.L.) exams.

MAGICAL GADGET: The Room of Requirement, a secret chamber in Hogwarts that appears to those in need of a space for hiding, meetings or storage
DEFENSE AGAINST THE DARK ARTS TEACHER: Dolores Umbridge, whose cruelty and refusal to teach the subject matter prompts Harry and the gang to form their own rogue Defense Against the Dark Arts group, Dumbledore's Army
NEW SPELL: The Protean Charm, which links objects together usefully for Dumbledore's Army
NUMBER OF PAGES: 896
WHAT HARRY LEARNS: That he will have to be the one to kill Voldemort, because according to the prophecy, "either must die at the hand of the other for neither can live while the other survives"

THE REVIEW: Rowling does so much right that it's churlish to dwell on her minor missteps. She has shed the clumsy devices—the impostors and the secret identities—that marred the shape of some of the earlier books. Her prose, always a serviceable, unshowy instrument, is stronger and more confident, and she has become a virtuoso plotter, a master at snappy pacing, able to stun and surprise at will. But what really makes the Harry Potter series great is its dual nature. It's a fantasy wrapped around a nightmare, an unreal, escapist fiction with an icy core of emotional pain that is very real.

Harry Potter and the Half-Blood Prince

THE PROBLEM: As Voldemort's power grows, Harry needs a crash course in everything it will take to stop him—and with Dumbledore's life under threat, he doesn't have much time to learn from the master
QUIDDITCH UPDATE! Harry is now captain of the Gryffindor squad
SCARY MONSTER: Zombie-like beings called Inferi
MAGICAL GADGET: The Horcrux, an object in which a Dark witch or wizard has stored a part of his or her soul after committing murder
DEFENSE AGAINST THE DARK ARTS TEACHER: Severus Snape; Horace Slughorn is Potions Master
NEW SPELL: The Unbreakable Vow; violate your

LOVE AND QUIDDITCH Sparks fly on the field.

THE GREAT ESCAPE *Deathly Hallows* begins with a callback to Book One: Hagrid fetching Harry on his motorbike.

enchanted promise and you die
NUMBER OF PAGES: 672
WHAT HARRY LEARNS: That Voldemort has split his soul into multiple Horcruxes, which Harry and his friends will have to find and destroy

THE REVIEW: For true believers, *Half-Blood Prince* will be pure pleasure. There's Quidditch, potion-class high jinks, apparition lessons, loads of snogging (Ron and Hermione are slowly sorting out their longtime mutual crush) and some lovely business with a golden potion called Felix Felicis that makes whoever imbibes it extra lucky. But this is the second-to-last book in the series, and for all the fun, the mood is darkening. You can't help but feel that Rowling is trotting out the fan favorites—your Tonks, your Luna, your Buckbeak, your Fred and George—for a final sunlit outing before chaos overtakes Harry.

Harry Potter and the Deathly Hallows

THE PROBLEM: Harry, Ron and Hermione have left Hogwarts on a quest to hunt Horcruxes. The fate of the world hangs in the balance
QUIDDITCH UPDATE! The first Golden Snitch Harry ever caught returns in a helpful capacity
SCARY MONSTER: Death itself
MAGICAL GADGET: The Deluminator, previously known as a tool to put out and turn on lights but now doing double duty as a homing device
DEFENSE AGAINST THE DARK ARTS TEACHER: Amycus Carrow, a Death Eater who makes students practice the Cruciatus Curse on each other
NEW SPELL: Fiendfyre, a cursed flame that seeks out living targets
NUMBER OF PAGES: 784
WHAT HARRY LEARNS: How to sacrifice himself for the cause—and that there can be life after death

THE REVIEW: As a farewell to the series, *Deathly Hallows* is everything fans of Harry Potter could hope for. It does not reach the lyrical high-water marks of the series. But then again, this isn't a lyrical interlude; this is the grand finale. It calls for big battles and high body counts, force majeure and not legerdemain, and Rowling leaves no stops unpulled.

We did something very rare for Harry Potter: we lost our cool. There is nothing particularly hip about loving Harry. He's not sexy or dangerous the way, say, Tony Soprano was. He's not an antihero, he's just a hero, but we fell for him anyway. We did and do love Harry. We couldn't help ourselves.

—Lev Grossman, Elizabeth Gleick, Sarah Begley, Paul Gray

The Stroke of Midnight

Readers in costume. Books hot off the press. Inside the mania of midnight release parties

BETWEEN 2000 AND 2007, THERE WERE ONLY two reasons a British or American kid might be allowed to stay up until midnight: to watch the ball drop on New Year's Eve and to attend a Harry Potter midnight book release party. (OK, maybe for a midnight screening of a Harry Potter movie, too—but more about that later.) They came in droves, miniature witches and wizards dressed in black robes, scarves striped the colors of their favorite Hogwarts house (but mostly scarlet and gold for Gryffindor), round glasses perched on their noses, wands in their hands, and lightning bolts drawn on their foreheads with face paint or, in a pinch, Mom's eyeliner. They queued up, played games, grew dizzy with excitement until the clock struck 12 and they could finally get what they came for.

The only question remaining: Would their parents let them stay up late into the night reading the precious novel? Or would they have to sneak a flashlight into bed—*Lumos!*—to continue the adventure? —*Sarah Begley*

IN THE MOMENT The trend was revived in 2016 with the script for *Harry Potter and the Cursed Child*. Clockwise from top: Fans lined up at Waterstones in Piccadilly, London, in 2016; shoppers at Bookies in Denver in 2003; German fans in Potsdam in 2003; a Gryffindor at the Scholastic Store in New York in 2007.

Harry Potter
AND THE
DEATHLY
HALLOWS

OUTSIDE THE BOX Some fans get inventive when it comes to costuming. Clockwise from left: A girl dressed as a snowy owl (like Hedwig) at a Borders in Marietta, Ga., in 2007; fans went fancy at a launch party at Edinburgh Castle in 2005; face paint added pizzazz at the Scholastic Store in 2007.

FILM SCHOOL Hogwarts's exterior in the movies (shown here in a film still) was built to scale in a British studio; the interior is based on Christ Church College at Oxford.

Screen Magic

MOVIE ADAPTATIONS DON'T ALWAYS LIVE UP TO THE expectations book lovers set for them, and the stakes are especially high for fantasy series. Fans demand fidelity to complicated texts; studios demand a clean two-to-three-hour edit. The tension of intent can hamstring a film. But by and large, the Harry Potter movies all hit the mark. As Richard Corliss wrote in TIME after the final film, they were "often so much better than good ... We may have ended our journey, but the films will dwell like a house elf in our hearts."

Readers, too, have lauded the faithful depiction of Hogwarts and its denizens throughout the franchise's life, and if there wasn't time for every shred of plot and exposition that made the books so captivating, there was certainly awe and entertainment in seeing the invisibility cloak, the talking paintings, the ghosts and the Gringotts goblins. Before long, children found their bedtimes extended again, this time for midnight *movie* release parties at local cinemas. Rows upon rows of tiny witches and wizards in their robes and scarves snacked on their Chocolate Frogs and Bertie Bott's Every Flavor Beans and gazed up as the magic unfolded in a new way, at once familiar and exhilarating. —*Sarah Begley*

How Not to Spoil a Plot

An inside look at the elaborate secrecy campaign around the largest book printing of all time

BY LEV GROSSMAN AND ANDREA SACHS

YOU MIGHT THINK THE MOST IMPORTANT PRODuct that the publisher Scholastic released when it came to Harry Potter was a book. But you would be wrong. Each book was merely a byproduct, the catalyst for something else. The real product, the one that had kids and adults alike lined up at bookstores for that midnight release, is something that Scholastic executives call, in hushed, reverential tones, "the magic moment."

It is the moment of ineffable, intangible ecstasy that occurs when a reader opens his or her brand-new $34.99 copy of *Deathly Hallows*, or *Azkaban*, or any other in the franchise, for the first time. "All the way through the process, everybody who touches this [manuscript] has the same goal in mind," says Arthur A. Levine, Rowling's editor. "Midnight. Kids."

The magic moment is a rare and delicate thing: it occurs only when the reader comes to the book in a state of pure ignorance, with no advance knowledge of its contents. For the magic moment to happen, the theory goes, the reader's mind must be preserved in a state of absolute innocence: it must be spoiler-free. So to preserve the magic moment against informational contamination—via the Web or watercooler conversation or the Rita Skeeters of the global media—Scholastic created an infrastructure around the material unlike anything the publishing world had ever seen.

Take the extraordinarily plotted release in 2007 of the seventh and final book, *Deathly Hallows*, which at 12 million copies in the U.S. alone was the largest first printing of any book in history. Every Tuesday, roughly a dozen people gathered in a conference room on the sixth floor of Scholastic's headquarters in Manhattan. They were members of the Harry Potter brain trust. The group included, among others, Levine; Lisa Holton, president of

THE BIG THRILL A Los Angeles–area fan rips the wrapping off embargoed copies of *Deathly Hallows*.

Scholastic's trade division; Scholastic's art director and its heads of sales, marketing, production, communications and manufacturing; and the company's vice president and deputy general counsel, Mark Seidenfeld. "This room is really the most paranoid room," says Holton. "We don't talk to our children and spouses for months."

The seriousness with which the members of the Harry Potter brain trust regard their collective mission cannot be overstated. "We have always known that the series is already a modern classic," Holton says. "If you think about it in terms of literature, I can't think of another series—not just in children's literature but in adult—that does what J.K. Rowling does. Even Dickens doesn't come close."

The job of the Harry Potter brain trust begins when Rowling's creative process ends. In the case of *Deathly Hallows*, that happened on Jan. 11, 2007, when Rowling wrote the very last word of the Harry Potter saga in a suite at the Balmoral Hotel in Edinburgh. The task of traveling to England to pick up the manuscript fell to Seidenfeld. To make absolutely sure the manuscript was safe on the plane, he sat on it.

But he didn't read it. Even up through the book's release, very few people at Scholastic had

had any actual contact with the contents of *Deathly Hallows*—"a handful," according to Kyle Good, the head of communications. Among that handful was Levine, who edited the most famous writer in the world. ("She's very strong, but she's not blind," he says. "She seems really to value when we ask her questions. She'll say, 'Oh, I knew what that was in my mind, but if it's not coming across that way, why don't we say *x*.' ") Another early reader was a studious young woman named Cheryl Klein, whose job title was continuity editor. Rowling's books have become so complex—and their fans so obsessively nitpicky—that it takes a full-time Potterologist to make sure Rowling's fictional universe stayed factually consistent. "I keep track of all of the various proper nouns that appear in the series," says Klein. "For instance, with Bertie Bott's Every Flavor Beans, I make sure it's always B-o-t-t-apostrophe-s. Every Flavor is not hyphenated, and Flavor does not have a u." It was a tough beat: Klein acknowledges, for example, that in *Harry Potter and the Chamber of Secrets*, Moaning Myrtle sits in a U-bend toilet, whereas in *Harry Potter and the Goblet of Fire*, she occupies an S-bend toilet (this crept in, it should be noted, before Klein's tenure, which began after *Goblet*). Klein had either the worst job in the world or the best, depending on how you look at it.

Like everyone else at Scholastic, Klein maintained the Harry Potter omertà. "Most people know better than to ask," she says. "That includes my friends and my family and everyone else." After Rowling revised the manuscript, per Levine's and Klein's suggestions, Klein flew to England to pick up the new draft. On her way home she was stopped for a random security check at Heathrow Airport. "The woman opens up my bag, and she starts pawing through it. And she says, 'Wow! You have a lot of paper here.' And I thought, Oh God, she's going to look at it, and she's going to see the names Harry and Ron and Hermione. But I just smiled, and I said, 'Yes, a lot of paper!' And she said, 'Uh-huh,' and

The Epic Saga of the Seventh Manuscript

Or, how the supersecret final Potter tale went from finished draft to hardcover book in 10 very careful, complicated steps

1. Rowling, who dreamed up Harry while on a train from Manchester to London, finishes the story on Jan. 11, 2007. The final book weighs in at 784 pages.

2. Scholastic lawyer Mark Seidenfeld picks up the pages in England. For safekeeping, he uses the manuscript as a seat cushion all the way back to the U.S.

5. Back to Rowling. Editors' notes in hand, she revises the first draft, then hands it off to her agent, Christopher Little ...

6. ... who orchestrates another handoff to Klein, who has flown to England for the mission. "I felt very special. I felt like I had a secret," she says. Klein's cover is almost blown when she is stopped by airport security.

7. Klein gets the manuscript safely back to Scholastic. What happens in that chamber of secrets and at the presses is the process that shall not be named.

she zipped it up. That was the end of the scariest two minutes of my life."

At first the number of copies of the *Deathly Hallows* manuscript was kept to an absolute minimum. One went to the book's designer. Also admitted to the inner circle was Mary GrandPré, the Florida-based artist who illustrated the U.S. editions. (If you've seen the English cover for *Deathly Hallows*, you know how lucky Americans are to have GrandPré.) "She is a wonderful lady," Good says. "She had an image of what Harry Potter looked like, but when she went to actually draw his face, she was really having a lot of trouble. She had the messy hair, the glasses, but what did his jawline look like? She walked over and she looked in the mirror, and she sketched her own face."

As GrandPré studied her jawline in the mirror for inspiration, the heavy industrial gears of the Harry Potter engine were beginning to grind up north. The more copies of a book a publisher prints, the more security issues multiply, and this was a record printing. The threat to the magic moment became quite real. In 2003 a forklift driver at a British printing plant was caught hawking pages from *Harry Potter and the Order of the Phoenix*. A month before *Harry Potter and the Half-Blood Prince* went on sale, two men were arrested in England for trying to sell a copy to a reporter; one of them served 4 ½ years. As a result, Scholastic won't give out the locations of the printing plants it uses or even how many there are. (As for Bloomsbury, the series' British publisher, it fiercely denied a rumor that it forced factory workers to print *Deathly Hallows* in pitch darkness.) The finished books travel to stores on pallets sealed in black plastic, in trucks tracked by GPS.

But Scholastic's protection can extend only so far, and once the books are delivered, security is in the hands of bookstore owners, all of whom signed a long, tightly worded legal agreement requiring them to keep the boxes unopened until 12:01 a.m. on July 21. "No one here sees them,"

3. Seidenfeld hands off copies of the draft to Arthur A. Levine (Rowling's American editor) and Cheryl Klein (the Potterologist), who look for problems.

4. Meanwhile, artist Mary GrandPré reads a copy and works her end of the magic, crafting illustrations. She has called the Harry Potter books a "candy store for an illustrator."

8. *Potter* is printed—somewhere. The record-breaking first run of 12 million dwarfs the number for the first novel: initially a mere 50,000 made it to stores.

9. In GPS-tracked boxes toted by FedEx, the books fan out across the country. To limit leakage, millions of copies arrive at bookstores within an eight-hour window.

10. On July 21, 2007, at 12:01 a.m., the magic moment happened, delaying bedtimes around America, for the sake of the pleasure of reading.

says Kim Brown, formerly vice president of merchandising at Barnes & Noble, which hired an outside security firm to guard the padlocked trucks in which it stores its copies of *Deathly Hallows*. Sean Sundwall, then at Amazon.com, said his company cordoned off a special area for Potter books. "Only a very small number of people are allowed to look at it—or breathe on it—and even a smaller number of people can touch it."

That's all well and good for the big players, but libraries and smaller bookstores aren't set up for Azkaban-level security. "The boxes say HARRY POTTER on them, so people get all excited," says Dana Harper, who co-owned Brystone Children's Books in Fort Worth, Tex., with her mother and sister. "Behind the counter, we have them covered with a cloth before we cut into them, just in case. We do get nervous that someone will break in, but that hasn't happened yet."

For owners of small businesses, trapped between the demands of millions of ravenous fans and those of a large corporation protecting a major asset, the experience can be disconcerting. "I can't even tell you where the books will be!" says Liz Murphy, former owner of the Learnéd Owl Book Shop in Hudson, Ohio. "We had to sign our life away."

It's all in the service of that magic moment, when readers turned the first page of what Rowling swears will be the last Harry Potter novel ever published. If the goal of Scholastic's strenuous secrecy campaign was to turn the release of *Deathly Hallows* into an event comparable to the premiere of a movie or the series finale of a beloved TV show, then by all means, the mischief was managed, with more than a whiff of "Who shot J.R.?" in the air and

COUNTING THE MINUTES Above, a New York bookstore display features a countdown to the release of a new Harry Potter book. Opposite, a steamer trunk containing the first author-signed copy of *Half-Blood Prince* is unloaded outside Scholastic headquarters.

A hacker calling himself "Gabriel" announced on a website that he had done exactly what the Harry Potter brain trust most feared: stolen the text of *Deathly Hallows.*

a satisfying sense that the written word for once got the hype usually accorded only to hipper and newer-fangled media. "If they're toward the counter when the boxes are sliced into," says Harper, "you might hear a sort of screaming or some oohs and ahs and breaths being taken in."

But with all that emphasis on the magic moment, there was a risk that people would forget why books are, in fact, books—not movies or TV shows. They're not about midnight parties or hype or even moments, however magical. Reading is, after all, the most solitary and contemplative and long-lasting of all aesthetic pleasures. "We'd just like to sell it like other books," Harper admits, a little wearily. "Just get it in and sell it. It can be kind of a circus." If Harry were real, he would find all the fuss intensely embarrassing. After all, if all readers cared about was the outcomes, then why would they turn out in such numbers to see the movie versions of the books, the fifth of which (*Harry Potter and the Order of the Phoenix*) hit cinemas 10 days before the seventh book was published.

Ironically, the Harry Potter brain trust could be guilty of underestimating the power of the books it worked so energetically to sell. The magic-moment strategy promotes a myth about Rowling's work—and reading in general—which is that the pleasure of a book is a fragile enchantment that's easily dispelled. On June 20, 2007, a hacker calling himself "Gabriel" announced on a website that he had done exactly what the Harry Potter brain trust most feared: stolen the text of *Deathly Hallows*. Explaining that he had gained access to a Bloomsbury employee's computer using an email-borne Trojan-horse program, he posted what he claimed were key plot points from the book. He framed his actions as a Christian counterattack against a work that promoted the "Neo-Paganism faith." Quoth Gabriel: "We make this spoiler to make reading of the upcoming book useless and boring."

The spoilers turned out to be fake. Gabriel didn't offer a shred of evidence supporting their authenticity, and anyway, boasting about things that you haven't actually done is pretty much what hacker culture is all about. But even if the spoilers had been genuine, it wouldn't have mattered.

On this point, both hacker and publisher share a key misunderstanding of what reading is all about. People read books for any number of reasons; finding out how the story ends is one among many. If it were otherwise, nobody would ever bother to read a book twice. Reading is about spending time with characters and entering a fictional world and playing with words and living through a story page by page. The idea that someone could ruin a novel by revealing its ending is like saying you could ruin the *Mona Lisa* by revealing that it's a picture of a woman with a center part. Spoilers are a myth: they don't spoil. No elaborate secrecy campaign could make *Harry Potter and the Deathly Hallows* any better than it already is, and no website could possibly make it useless and boring.

Box-Office Gold

The films cast a spell on audiences and on critics

BY RICHARD CORLISS

HOW TO MAKE A FILM OUT OF SUCH A CINEMATIC experience that more than 400 million readers have seen it in their minds' eye? Either by transferring it, like a lavishly illustrated volume of Dickens, or transforming it with a new vision. An adapter of a famous work need not choose between fidelity and poetry; the King James version of the Bible has both.

Beyond its longevity records and the billions it has amassed in revenues, the Harry Potter series is a proud, mammoth act of commercial, communal filmmaking. It's Hollywood at its finest, though the setting, accent, ensemble cast and most of the creative team are distinctly English. This is highly intelligent blockbuster filmmaking, and by the end one can clap the completed series on its figurative back and pronounce a hearty "Well done."

FLASHING LIGHTS At the *Deathly Hallows: Part 1* premiere in 2010. Opposite: the *Phoenix* premiere in 2007

Harry Potter and the Sorcerer's Stone

With *Harry Potter and the Sorcerer's Stone*, director Chris Columbus bravely goes toe to toe with the imagination of readers who have purchased 450 million Potter books and made the boy wizard one of the most beloved figures in literary history. The big-screen adaptation is a film of such eye-popping grandeur, dazzling special effects and sumptuous production values that you may not notice right away that supporting characters like Peeves, a troublesome ghost, and Piers, a troublesome boy, have been given the heave-ho.

Of all the directors in the running, including *City of Angels*'s Brad Silberling and *Dead Man Walking*'s Tim Robbins, Columbus had the sappiest rep after his most recent movies, *Bicentennial Man* and *Stepmom*. But he also had two *Home Alone* movies to his credit, which meant that he knew how to work with child actors. Another plus: earlier in his career, as a screenwriter, Columbus penned the wickedly subversive action comedy *Gremlins*, which was a hit for Warner Bros. in 1984. Columbus admits that as a director, "I was going down this soft, sentimental road ... I'm the guy who wrote *Gremlins*. I tried to find something after I finished *Bicentennial* that would go back to that *Gremlins* area." Despite his A-list status in Hollywood, Columbus agreed to audition for the job by pitching himself to the studio. Producer David Heyman says Columbus was hired ultimately because of his "desire to be faithful to the material."

Harry Potter and the Chamber of Secrets

"It's more of everything," Daniel Radcliffe, who plays Harry, told TIME of *Chamber of Secrets*. "And it's a lot darker." It is also much scarier. A dead cat is hung in a hallway at Hogwarts School of Witchcraft and Wizardry; children are frozen stiff (or "petrified") by a monster; Harry and his sidekick Ron (Rupert Grint) are attacked with surprising violence by a monstrous Whomping Willow after crash-landing in its gnarled branches in a flying car. Later, they're chased through the Forbidden Forest by an army of giant spiders.

EVOLUTIONARY THEORY As the movies progressed, with a series of different directors attached, the tone grew darker and the special effects (like those involving the Hippogriff, bottom right) grew much more sophisticated.

Warner Bros. was afraid that the movie would receive a PG-13 rating—a dangerous proposition, since Potter's most devoted fans are preteens. Just as important, the core consumers for Potter toys, which generated about $500 million in sales for *Sorcerer's Stone*, range in age from 7 to 11. Instead, the film is conveniently PG, like its predecessor.

Still, the filmmakers are eager to let you know that your children may be afraid, very afraid. "I would strongly caution parents," said Columbus, who also directed this installment, "anyone who has a 7-year-old or younger, to make sure they know what they're getting into."

Going into his second year at Hogwarts, Harry is more heroic, and so is Columbus. While he was accused of being too slavishly faithful to Rowling's book the first time around, in *Chamber of Secrets* the director gives his imagination freer rein. In the new film, Quidditch—the ball game played by young witches and wizards on broomsticks—is as exciting as a car chase. And it all adds up to a two-hour, 42-minute movie—nine minutes longer than *Sorcerer's Stone*. "The length didn't seem to be an issue last time," says Columbus, "but I wanted this film to feel as if it moved much quicker."

—*Jess Cagle*

Harry Potter and the Prisoner of Azkaban

Azkaban has one of the strongest plots in the canon thus far. Harry, now 13 and in his third year at Hogwarts, is challenged by the escape of the notorious Sirius Black from Azkaban, the Alcatraz of the wizardly world. With a new danger, a new protector: Defense Against the Dark Arts professor Lupin, a wise, kindly gent with the habit of disappearing every few weeks and then returning with unseemly scratches on his face. Aided by Hermione and Ron, Harry must discern protective friend from mortal foe at the risk of his life—and of learning astonishing things about himself.

For the third film, Chris Columbus handed the reins to Alfonso Cuarón, the Mexican director best known for the too-hot-for-an-R sex comedy *Y Tu Mamá También*. Cuarón, however, also made the English-language children's film *A Little Princess*, so he knows his way around precocious kid actors. Just about everything plays better this time. The production team, headed by designer Stuart Craig, stopped pausing to admire its handiwork and splashed splendid images on the screen at a brisk pace. *Azkaban* conjures up a purple triple-decker bus (it can instantly slim itself to pass between two vehicles), a Monster Book of Monsters (it snarls at Harry, then scoots under his bed) and Buckbeak the Hippogriff (a wonderfully realistic creature with an unpredictable personality). And does it all without preening.

Harry Potter and the Goblet of Fire

The *Goblet* movie gets bustling straight off, dense—every millimeter of screen space is art-directed up the wazoo—but not congested, Terry Gilliam–style. Each of the thousand elements knows its place: in the background, ceding eye-focus to the story and its increasingly plausible and compelling characters.

This time, Heyman and screenwriter Steve Kloves handed the directing job to Mike Newell, a Brit who has directed a few good, tense melodramas (*Dance with a Stranger*, *Donnie Brasco*) and some engaging sentimental fare (*Enchanted April*, *Four Weddings and a Funeral*). What does a new director do on a sustained enterprise like the Potter films (or the James Bonds)? My guess is that the man-for-hire attends to the film's pace and the care and feeding of the actors. Newell did an exemplary job here, encouraging and eliciting a community of performance.

The film's one unneeded plot strand concerns an estrangement between Ron and Harry. Why bother sundering them when we know they'll get back together?

Harry Potter and the Order of the Phoenix

In *Order of the Phoenix*, named after the secret society of rebels who began fighting Voldemort back when they were at Hogwarts, Harry starts his own student group, Dumbledore's Army, which in the DVD extras Radcliffe describes as "a guerrilla revolutionary organization." The adults—that glittering array of British acting royalty—still have meaty roles, with Imelda Staunton taking center stage this time as Dolores Umbridge, a steely commissar cocooned in soft pinks; director David Yates describes Umbridge as "a genetic splice between Doris Day and Freddy Krueger." But the spotlight is on the young stars, who have grown into their roles over the seven years and five films, especially Radcliffe, who has justified the faith the producers put in him when he was the age of Rowling's target readers.

By *Phoenix*, Harry is both a wizard Luke Skywalker (boy-man on a mission) and a melancholy Hamlet (a teen prince, all too aware of the forces roiling against him, and within him). He must face down Voldemort the way other boys confront puberty—as a threat and a thrill that run seismic changes and hormonal rage through his body. Wise beyond his years, Harry also seems prematurely tired, a wizened wizard at 15. And Radcliffe measures up to his character; his bold shadings reveal Harry as both a tortured adolescent and an epic hero ready to do battle.

Harry Potter and the Half-Blood Prince

The finishing order of *Half-Blood Prince*'s opening weekend—coming in over *Ice Age 3* and *Transformers 2*—might seem like the score of a three-team intergalactic Quidditch match, but it's really a demonstration of the power of sequels. The sixth installment of the Potter series earned more than $200 million worldwide in its first weekend. Numbers like those are the main reason Hollywood's slavish adherence to remaking its biggest hits won't change anytime soon. In the final films, the boy will grow into the holy warrior. Those climactic works couldn't have a stronger prelude than *Half-Blood Prince*—an evocation, not leering but knowing, of adolescence under siege.

HERE AND THERE Although most of the series takes place in enchanted locales, the characters sometimes had to venture into banal cityscapes.

Harry Potter and the Deathly Hallows: Part 1

The decision by Heyman (who produced all the films), Kloves (who scripted all but one) and Yates (who directed the last four of the eight) to cut the final book into two features, whatever its sense as a business strategy, meant slowing the story down just as it should rev up. Instead of scooting like a Golden Snitch during a Quidditch championship, *DH1* is struck with a long spell of aimlessness, and the viewer with the curse of ennui. This should be exciting: a treasure hunt, with the trio ever a hairsbreadth from betrayal and death. Now our hero is finally on his fateful quest, crossing paths with all manner of creatures—elves and goblins and Voldemort's pet snake—and steeling himself to cross wands with the Dark Lord. But Harry rarely goes questing. The film's movement is lateral, not forward, as Harry spends much of his time cursing his mentor Dumbledore, killed at the end of Episode 6, for not having left clearer clues to follow. The viewer feels the headmaster's absence just as acutely. Dumbledore's majesty, as incarnated by the great Michael Gambon, was fierce but soothing, his paternal love for Harry the strongest relationship in the series. With his Gandalf gone, Harry has to rely on his own suddenly skimpy resources. He seems less a hero than an ordinary, fretful 17-year-old. In other words, he's human. As Barack Obama could tell Harry, it's tough being anointed the Chosen One.

A SINGULAR VISION David Yates helmed the last four films, giving them a measure of consistency. He went on to direct *Fantastic Beasts and Where to Find Them*.

Harry Potter and the Deathly Hallows: Part 2

Kloves and Yates hurtle through Rowling's last 300 pages toward the big face-off. Essentially a war movie, *DH2* portrays the siege of Hogwarts as a children's crusade with late-blooming heroes. Now the vast sets have been dismantled, the cast and crew dispersed with final hugs and tearful thanks. We may have ended our journey, but the films will dwell like a house elf in our hearts and on that perpetual-memory machine, the TV. School's out, but we'll always have Hogwarts.

CHAPTER FIVE

A Cast of Characters

CASTING THE PARENTS AND PROFESSORS IN THE Harry Potter movies was a no-brainer: the filmmakers opted for a parade of Britain's best, with Royal Academy pedigrees and more than a dozen BAFTAs among them. But the youth roles posed special challenges. Besides finding kids who matched the physical descriptions, the filmmakers had to gamble on less experienced kids—they were just kids, after all!—and hope the actors would find the stamina to sustain a possible seven movies (which turned into eight).

From 2001 to 2011, moviegoers watched Daniel Radcliffe, Emma Watson, Rupert Grint and their young castmates age into young adults. And as these actors came into their own—setting their eyes on careers with trajectories beyond the series—their conversations with the press revealed how formative, not to mention very real, life at Hogwarts was for them.

"I will have been here for over a decade by the time we're done," Watson said in a 2010 interview. "It's been like my home, it's been my school, it's been like my family, it's been everything. Obviously I'll be very sad to leave so many people that I care about behind, but I'm also excited to do other things." —*Sarah Begley*

THREE'S COMPANY Radcliffe, Grint and Watson film *The Order of the Phoenix* in 2007. All were teenagers: Grint was 18, and the other two were 17.

Growing Up Potter

Daniel Radcliffe, Emma Watson and others talk about hitting the teen years on the set

BY LEV GROSSMAN

THE HARRY POTTER MOVIES WERE FILMED PRIMARILY at a former airplane factory 20 miles outside London. Inside Leavesden Studios, Harry Potter's past existed as a dreamlike mishmash: bits and pieces of the Whomping Willow, signs from the stores in Diagon Alley, the smashed-up remains of giant chess pieces from *Harry Potter and the Sorcerer's Stone*. Is this any place to raise a child?

When Daniel Radcliffe was cast as Harry, he was only 11 years old. Emma Watson (Hermione Granger) was 10; Rupert Grint (Ron Weasley), almost 12. By the time the fourth film, *Harry Potter and the Goblet of Fire*, opened, they had spent a third of their lives making movies, going from children to teenagers entirely within the weird, closed bubble of the Potterverse.

Already at age 16, Radcliffe seemed aware of what a strange childhood fate had consigned him to, but he wasn't that bothered by it. "I've got quite a surreal mind anyway, so I don't think it's made much difference to how I see everything," he said at the time. "That's what's weird: I don't think of it as being that bizarre."

When Warner Bros. set about filming the Harry Potter books, it wasn't exactly uppermost in everyone's mind that the company would essentially be opening a boarding school for child actors (who spent three hours a day with an on-set tutor). "When you start, you don't really anticipate that it will last seven

FEATHERED FRIEND Hedwig, Harry's pet snowy owl, was played by several birds.

films," said the movies' producer David Heyman late in the series. "It's like school, so you have people getting closer and people growing apart, but we've never had a fight." And what about puberty, a specter almost as unmentionable as He Who Must Not Be Named? "There are crushes and romances here and there," Heyman said then, "but nothing to do with the central characters. I've never caught anyone making out behind one of the backings or anything like that. I'm sure it's probably gone on, but I don't want to know about it."

While working on *Goblet*, director Mike Newell described shooting as a moving target. "I've just been working on a scene which we shot in our first week, and Dan still looks the little kid that he was in *Sorcerer's Stone*," said Newell, whose credits also include *Four Weddings and a Funeral*. "Eleven months later, he [didn't] look like that at all. And that scene of him comes two thirds of the way through the movie. So he starts as a kid of 15, then he gets younger, then he gets older, then he gets younger."

"There's never been a day when I've thought, 'I really don't want to be here,' " Radcliffe said. "For me, it's this or school. I've never really loved being in school that much."

"Mike really brings out how awkward and awful and how embarrassing the whole situation is," said Watson, then 15. "All of the younger actors played on their own experiences to make that feel as real as we could."

Social life on Planet Potter didn't always mirror that in J.K. Rowling's books. Radcliffe and Grint weren't very close on the first several films. "Rupert I don't know that well," Radcliffe said then. "Which is weird. I think it's partly because he finished school before I did. Emma, I do know exceptionally well. Very, very well." Um, so did they ever, like . . . you know? "No. But I had a big crush on her when I first met her, definitely. But she's more like a sister now."

Radcliffe's best friend at Leavesden was, at the time of *Goblet of Fire*, "Will Steggle, who's my—I hate to use the word, because I'll sound like a precocious child star—but he's credited as being my personal dresser. He is in actuality my best friend in the world. And he's 39. Which is upsetting, because he is so much older, and it means he's gonna die probably before me."

Life on set could be tough on adults too. The *Goblet of Fire* shoot took 11 months—an eternity in Hollywood time—partly because kids can legally work only four hours a day.

But, said Radcliffe at the time, "There's never been a day when I've thought, 'I really don't want to be here.' Because for me, it's this or it's school. And I've never really loved being in school that much."

If there was a real downside to growing up Potter, it may have been that the actors' adolescence was on display in multiplexes the world over, in excruciating close-up. "When you see [the film] sometimes you can think, 'Oh no, they used that bit!' " said Bonnie Wright, then 14, who played Ron's little sister Ginny. "I think everyone sometimes feels intimidated by themselves when they see themselves on the screen."

After all, it's hard enough figuring out who you are when you're a teenager. How much harder is it when you spend all day pretending to be someone else?

GROWING PAINS The cast were just tweens when shooting for the first film began. Together, they aged through the franchise, adults by the end.

Q&A

Daniel Radcliffe

1. How different are you from Harry?
I think I am probably quite different from Harry. [But] I think we're both quite reserved in terms of how much we show our feelings. Neither of us particularly wears our heart on our sleeve. The value of friendship in both our lives is immense. And I also think we have a shared curiosity.

2. What do you think has been Harry's greatest misstep or failure in judgment?
I think the way he treated his friends a couple of films ago was quite questionable. They're always there for him, and he was a little bit ungrateful. I think Harry is a flawed character. He can be quite selfish and really manipulative. He's not all sweetness and light.

3. The Harry Potter films have given you a chance to work with an extraordinary number of British acting royalty. Which ones have had the greatest effect on you?
The two that have had the biggest effect on me would be Gary Oldman, who I became very close to, and Imelda Staunton. They're both wonderful people and wonderful actors.

4. Both *Half-Blood Prince* and *Deathly Hallows* are quite different from previous installments. How have you prepared for darker, deeper scenes?
That's the kind of stuff I like doing and gravitate toward. It probably comes easier to me than the comedy. On those days, I generally try to be as isolated as possible and listen to lots of music that will hopefully kind of depress me or get me into a less exuberant state.

5. If you could use any of the magical spells from Harry Potter, which would you choose?
It's not a spell, but if I could choose any magical thing, it would definitely be the lucky potion. If you have too much, apparently, it screws you up, but the idea of having that perfect day is just so wonderful.

6. Are you a Harry Potter fan?
I am a fan of the books, certainly. In terms of the films, I enjoy watching everyone but myself very, very much. I don't like watching myself. I don't think many actors do. But, yeah, I am a fan. If I weren't, I would've stopped ages ago.

7. What do you think about the way J.K. Rowling formed the plots of the books?
Obviously, it's inspired. Otherwise they wouldn't have done nearly as well as they have. They have taken the best bits of different kinds of literature. There's the English boarding school. There's the good-vs.-evil thing. The fact that she came up with the entire thing on one train journey is pretty remarkable.

8. Would you ever commit to the lead role in a movie series again?
I think it would be a while, at least, before I did that. It would have to be very good. *—July 2009*

Emma Watson

1. What do you like most and least about your character, Hermione Granger?

I love that she has an opinion, that she's intelligent, that she has a heart. Things I dislike: she's a little bossy, a little mothering—which I'm sure could get very irritating.

2. Is it true that someone yelled "10 points to Gryffindor" after you answered something correctly when you were a student at Brown?

That has never happened to me. Maybe someone said it under their breath, but I've never, ever had anyone say that when I've been in a class.

3. Would you consider a profession outside of acting?

The difficulty for me is that I'm interested in so many different things. I could never really imagine myself doing one thing, and I'm pretty sure that I'll end up doing four or five different things. I want to be a Renaissance woman. I want to paint, and I want to write, and I want to act, and I want to just do everything.

4. Which Harry Potter movie has been your favorite to work on?

I've enjoyed all of them in different ways. I think the first one was incredible, obviously, because everything was new, and everything being a novelty is very exciting. From an acting perspective, this last movie was amazing because I had such big parts, and it was really challenging and demanding. I did a lot of stunts and had a lot of very difficult scenes to do.

5. What was the last day of filming the final film like?

It was really emotional. It almost felt like an out-of-body experience because it's been coming for such a long time. I felt like I had spoken about it so much and thought about it so much, but when it actually arrived, it just didn't feel real. It was very hard to process.

6. What is your favorite book and why?

My dad read me *The BFG*, by Roald Dahl, when I was younger. I'm really fond of that book. *Le Petit Prince* [by Antoine de Saint-Exupéry]. I like books that aren't just lovely but that have memories in themselves. Just like playing a song, picking up a book again that has memories can take you back to another place or another time.

7. You had doubts about continuing to play Hermione after the fifth movie. How would your life have been altered if you had not returned to the role?

I probably would have been public enemy No. 1. I would have found it very difficult watching the movies being made without me as a part of them, because I grew up making them. Being a part of this film franchise feels like part of my identity in a way. I would have gotten a lot more sleep. But I definitely made the right decision. *—November 2010*

In Their Own Words

Cast members sound off on the characters they played through the years

COMMITTING TO THE HARRY POTTER SERIES AS an actor meant playing the same character for a decade. To some, this was bliss—a role to dig into at length, steady work and a solid paycheck. Others, as interviews increasingly revealed, were quite ready to move on to new things by the time the franchise finale wrapped, though they still shed a few tears on the last day of filming.

Appearing in Harry Potter wasn't only an unusually long-term big-screen gig; it was also a game changer for many of the actors in their interactions with a public that would come to adore them. When they left the set, the child stars returned to curious classmates and the adults headed home to their own enthusiastic kids and grandkids eager to hear about their favorite franchise. All of the actors had to deal on some level with hordes of fans clamoring for autographs or photos (later, selfies). When it was time to audition for new projects, some actors had a hard time shaking off their Potter reputations and landing roles that defied expectations.

Over the years, in interviews with various publications and networks, the actors who animate these beloved characters have shared how they came to inhabit our imaginations—and how the experience changed their lives. —*Sarah Begley*

"A phone call with Jo Rowling, containing one small clue, persuaded me that there was more to Snape than an unchanging costume and that even though only three of the books were out at that time, she held the entire massive but delicate narrative in the surest of hands."

—ALAN RICKMAN (Prof. Severus Snape), April 2011

"I'd already won a Ron Weasley look-alike competition in a newspaper, so I thought I had a chance."

—**RUPERT GRINT** (Ron Weasley), July 2011

"I have ... never read a Harry Potter book. If you are an actor, all you have is the script you are given. If you read the book, you might get disappointed about what's been left out."

—**MICHAEL GAMBON** (Prof. Albus Dumbledore #2), September 2009

"I feel very lucky and pleased that when we were filming Harry Potter, social media didn't really exist."

—**BONNIE WRIGHT** (Ginny Weasley), October 2016

"In this business, it's so transitory—it's just 10 weeks here or there on a movie, and then it's over—but to see the same people over all that time, a decade, makes you feel really safe and secure."

—HELENA BONHAM CARTER (Bellatrix Lestrange), November 2011

"Sometimes you can create a character off a real-life person, but often you create something out of yourself. As it turned out, I very much had a part in the way he looked. I found little physicalities in the role, and something always happened when I put those long, flowing robes on. That's when I felt Voldemort."

—RALPH FIENNES (Lord Voldemort), July 2011

"The important thing, obviously, is to tell the story as it was. Because the children will soon let you know if you messed that thing up."

—**ROBBIE COLTRANE** (Prof. Rubeus Hagrid), February 2004

"A lot of very small people kind of used to say hello to me ... One kid once said to me, 'Were you really a cat?' And I heard myself saying, 'Just pull yourself together. How could I have been?' "

—**MAGGIE SMITH** (Prof. Minerva McGonagall), October 2013

"[My granddaughter] said, 'Papa, I hear you're not going to be in the Harry Potter movie,' and she said, 'If you don't play Dumbledore, then I will never speak to you again.' "

—**RICHARD HARRIS** (Prof. Albus Dumbledore #1), September 2001

"It's a bad idea to tell your 10-year-old to talk to me, because the poor child makes no connection with Mad-Eye Moody and he's looking at me saying, 'Why am I being asked to talk to a stranger?' "

—**BRENDAN GLEESON** (Mad-Eye Moody), August 2011

The New Star of the Wizarding World

As Newt Scamander in *Fantastic Beasts*, Eddie Redmayne will be a serial fixture on the big screen

BY MEGAN McCLUSKEY

EDDIE REDMAYNE IS STANDING WITH HIS TOES pointed out and his heels together. He picks up his right foot and very gingerly sets it down in front of him at the same awkward angle as it started, without creating any sound. "When you track a creature," he explains, "if there are twigs and leaves and you don't want to make a noise, you have to put one foot down as slowly as you can."

Newt Scamander was described to him as a character who walks his own walk. Redmayne plays the eccentric magizoologist—screenwriter J.K. Rowling's word for a witch or wizard who studies magical creatures—in *Fantastic Beasts and Where to Find Them*, the Harry Potter prequel set amid the social and political upheaval of New York City in the 1920s. Sitting with Redmayne at the Wooly, the retro-style speakeasy in the basement of Manhattan's Woolworth Building (which in the film serves as the Magical Congress of the United States of America), is like time-traveling to that era.

Armed with an enchanted briefcase—in which the beasts under his care live—Newt arrives in Manhattan planning to complete a global research expedition before returning home to Europe. But when a chance encounter with a No-Maj, the American term for a nonmagical person, leads to the escape of several of his animal wards, he finds himself embroiled in a centuries-long conflict between the wizarding world and its secular counterpart.

Playing a wand-waving vagabond who spends his time studying imaginary creatures is by no means Redmayne's usual shtick. In fact, the family-friendly *Fantastic Beasts* franchise—which is set to span five movies in all—is the first multi-installment series for the actor, 35, best known for starring in a string of critically acclaimed one-shots over the past few years, the most famous of which were grounded in actual history. Those roles have included Lili Elbe in *The Danish Girl*, which earned Redmayne a Best Actor nomination at the Oscars, and Stephen Hawking in *The Theory of Everything*, for which he won in the same category.

The shift to lighter subject matter brought no change in Redmayne's preparation, though. A Method actor, he researched the role by going into the field. "I went to a wildlife park," he says, "and met people who care for animals and watched all the idiosyncrasies of both how the animals behave and how the people who look after them behave."

On its face, the action of *Fantastic Beasts* centers on a practical matter: Newt's quest to retrieve his creatures. But on a deeper level, it explores the themes of intolerance and otherness that figure prominently in Rowling's seven-book Potter series. Our British hero struggles to understand the American laws that call for complete separation of the magical and nonmagical communities, a practice he without hesitation condemns as "backwards."

Redmayne says Rowling's ability to craft narratives that are entertaining but carry a message was a big part of the project's appeal for him. "She's weaving in bigger themes of repression and seg-

"The script just did something really special that I thought was unique. There was high comedy, and yet it left me really emotional."

regation," he says, "but manages to touch on them with a lightness that sticks with you afterward."

"You can only go on one's instinct for these things, and for me, it normally tends to be a physical reaction. I felt it in *The Theory of Everything* and similarly in this." That gut feeling was what ultimately persuaded him to take on this ambitious commitment. "The script just did something really special that I thought was really unique," he says. "It was all these different genres somehow—there was high comedy, and yet it left me really emotional."

Of course, there's also the allure of being inducted into the much beloved Potterverse—a global phenomenon since the release of Rowling's first novel in the summer of 1997. Callbacks to Potter's story are scattered throughout *Fantastic Beasts*, references that gave Redmayne a strong sense of nostalgia while reading Rowling's screenplay. "It had all this familiarity and the names of characters you've heard of and relatives of various protagonists from the Potter films," he says, "but in something that felt like its own thing."

Redmayne has his own ideas as to why the lore of Rowling's creation appeals so broadly. "I think all of us love escapism," he says. "The idea that there is a magical world running simultaneous to ours that is somewhere we can escape from the daily grind is kind of wonderful." *Beasts* comes on the heels of other Rowling releases that have renewed fan excitement—*Cursed Child* news, some short stories—but it's the first opportunity audiences have had to return to the big-screen wizarding world in more than five years.

For his part, Redmayne is confident in his quirky protagonist's ability to enchant both new and returning viewers. "You realize he has great passion and qualities that don't immediately seem heroic," he says, "but a heart that's quite heroic." Put it this way: Newt's walk may look different, but it's clearly within Redmayne's stride.

TIME TRAVELER Redmayne is taking the Potter universe backward and forward at the same time.

CHAPTER SIX

Across the Potterverse

TWENTY YEARS AFTER THE WORLD MET HARRY POTTER, his influence lives on in deeply personal ways. Character names like "Hermione" have spiked in popularity for newborns. Pets have been named Dobby and Winky and Fang and Crookshanks. Friends have gathered for their own versions of the Yule Ball, complete with homemade Butterbeer. College students have organized gravity-bound Quidditch leagues. Grand-gesture marriage proposals and lavish weddings have revolved around Harry Potter themes. Fans have tattooed themselves with icons like the Deathly Hallows symbol, or inspirational quotes from the books or movies. An especially popular quote choice: "Happiness can be found, even in the darkest of times, if one only remembers to turn on the light."

There's no doubt Harry Potter has had a massive influence on pop culture. But so, too, have cultural shifts influenced the ever-evolving world of Harry Potter. In a sign of the times, Rowling revealed in 2007 that Dumbledore was gay. More recently, a black actress was cast as Hermione in the London play *Harry Potter and the Cursed Child*. With four more *Fantastic Beasts* movies on the way and a Broadway version of *Cursed Child* hitting the U.S. next year, there are plenty more plot twists in store. —*Sarah Begley*

Outing Dumbledore

J.K. Rowling brought a beloved character out of the closet—but it was a complicated triumph

BY JOHN CLOUD

WHEN J.K. ROWLING ANNOUNCED AT CARNEGIE Hall in October 2007 that Albus Dumbledore—her Aslan, her Gandalf, her Yoda—was gay, the crowd apparently sat in silence for a few seconds and then burst into wild applause. I'm still sitting in silence.

Yes, it's nice that gays finally got a major character in the sci-fi/fantasy universe. Until Dumbledore, we had been shut out of the major franchises. J.R.R. Tolkien wrote a rich supply of homoeroticism into *The Lord of the Rings*—all those men and hobbits and elves singing to one another during long, womanless quests. The books and their film versions feature tender scenes between Frodo and Samwise. But in the end, Sam marries Rosie and fathers 13 children. Thirteen! Got something to prove, hobbit?

Other fantasy worlds have presented gay (or at least gay-seeming) characters, but usually they are, literally, inhuman. George Lucas gave us the epicene C-3PO and the little butch R2-D2, and their Felix-Oscar dialogue suggests the banter of a couple of old queens who have been keeping intergalactic house for millennia. But their implied homosexuality is quite safe. There is no real flesh that could actually entangle. Similarly, there was a girl-on-girl plot in 1995 on *Star Trek: Deep Space Nine*, but let me spare you a fanboy summary by noting that the two girls weren't girls (they were gender-non-binary aliens called Trills), and they only kissed.

So along comes Rowling with Dumbledore—a human being, a wizard even, an indisputable hero and one of the most beloved figures in children's literature. Shouldn't I be happy to learn he's gay?

Yes, except: Why couldn't he tell us himself? The Potter books add up to more than 800,000 words before Dumbledore dies in *Harry Potter and the Half-Blood Prince*, yet Rowling couldn't spare two of those words to help define a central character's emotional identity: "I'm gay." We can only conclude that Dumbledore saw his homosexuality as shameful. His silence suggests a lack of personal integrity that is completely out of character.

I had always given the Potter books a pass on the lack of gay characters because, especially at first, they were intended for little kids. But particularly with the appearance of the long, violent later books, Rowling allowed her witches and wizards to grow up, to get zits and begin romances, to kill and die. It seemed odd that not even a minor student character at Hogwarts was gay, especially since Rowling was so politically correct about inventing magical creatures of different races and species, incomes, national origins and developmental abilities. In a typical passage, Blaise Zabini is described as a "tall black boy with high cheekbones and long, slanting eyes." Would it have been so difficult to write a line in which Zabini takes the exquisitely named Justin Finch-Fletchley to the Yule Ball?

And then there's Dumbledore himself. Sure, he's heroic. His twinkling eyes, his flowing manteau, his unfailing wisdom: Rowling made it impossible not to revere him. But here is a gay man as desexed as any priest—and, to uncomfortably

extend the analogy, whose greatest emotional bond is with an adolescent boy: scarred, orphaned, needy Harry. Rowling said that in her conception of his character, Dumbledore had fallen in love with Gellert Grindelwald long ago, when the two were just teenagers. But Grindelwald turned out to be evil—Rowling's Hitler, in fact—which apparently broke Dumbledore's heart.

As far as we know, Dumbledore had no fully realized romance in all his 115 years—just a lifetime spent around children and, for the seven years we know him, a fascination with the boy Potter. That's pathetic and frustratingly stereotypical. It's difficult to believe someone as wise and sane as Dumbledore couldn't find at least one wizard his age to take to the Three Broomsticks.

Am I making too much of this? Undoubtedly. Some of the best *Star Trek* fan fiction involves steamy Kirk-Spock love affairs. So it will be with the Potter world, as Rowling has acknowledged. We are now all free to imagine a gay life more whole and fulfilling than the one Rowling gave Dumbledore. But it would have been better if she had just let the old fellow rest in peace.

How Harry Can Live Forever

Inside the alternate universe of fan fiction, where the Potter tales never end

BY LEV GROSSMAN

J.K. ROWLING SAYS SHE ISN'T GOING TO WRITE any more Harry Potter books. That doesn't mean there won't be more. It just means they won't be written by J.K. Rowling. Instead they'll be written by people like Racheline Maltese.

Maltese is 44. She's an actor and a professional writer—journalism, cultural criticism, fiction, poetry. She describes herself as queer. She lives in New York City. She's a fan of Harry Potter. Sometimes she writes stories about Harry and the other characters from the Potterverse and posts them online for free. "For me, it's sort of like an acting or improvisation exercise," Maltese says. "You have known characters. You apply a set of given circumstances to them. Then you wait and see what happens."

Maltese is a writer of fan fiction: stories and novels that make use of the characters and settings from other people's professional creative work. Fan fiction is what literature might look like if it were reinvented from scratch after a nuclear apocalypse by a band of brilliant pop-culture junkies trapped in a sealed bunker. They don't do it for money. That's not what it's about. The writers write it and put it

COLLAGE BY JO LYNN ALCORN

et slip in his excitement, for wha
e. However, he had the sense never to try a
charmed so many of my colleagues.
he moved up the school, he gathe
dedicated friends; I call them that, for w
lthough as I have already indicated, Riddle u
fection for any of them. This group had a kind
within the castle. They were a motley collection; a
said Hagrid, fat tear
nd trickling down in
bin me home since I w
me ter teach 'em, I'll
marble staircase
eral bewigged wi

up online just for the satisfaction. They're fans, but they're not silent, couch-bound consumers of media. The culture talks to them, and they talk back to the culture in its own language.

Right now fan fiction is still the cultural equivalent of dark matter: it's largely invisible to the mainstream, but at the same time, it's massive. Fan fiction predates the Internet, but the Web made it exponentially easier to talk and be heard, and it holds hundreds of millions of words of fan fiction. There's fan fiction based on books, movies, TV shows, video games, plays, musicals, rock bands and board games. There's fan fiction based on the Bible. FanFiction.net, the largest archive on the Web (though only one of many), hosts millions of pieces of fan fiction, ranging in length from short-short stories to full-length novels. The Harry Potter section alone contains more than 83,000 entries.

With the exception of E.L. James, whose *Twilight* fan fiction became *Fifty Shades of Grey*, fan fiction creators aren't making money from it. Whether anybody loses money on fan fiction is a separate question. The people who create the works that fan fiction borrows from are sharply divided on it. Rowling and Stephenie Meyer have given Harry Potter and *Twilight* fan fiction their blessing; if anything, fan fiction has acted as a viral marketing agent for their work. Other writers consider it a violation of their copyrights and, more, of their emotional claim to their own creations. They feel as if their characters have been kidnapped by strangers.

On FanFiction.net, the Harry Potter section alone contains more than 83,000 entries, many of them full-length novels.

You can see both sides of the issue. Do characters belong to the person who created them? Or to the fans who love them so passionately that they spend their nights and weekends laboring to extend those characters' lives, for free? There's a division here, a geological fault line, that looks small on the surface but runs deep into our culture, and the tectonic plates are only moving further apart. Is art about making up new things or about transforming the raw material that's out there? Cutting, pasting, sampling, remixing and mashing up have become mainstream modes of cultural expression, and fan fiction is part of that. It challenges just about everything we thought we knew about art and creativity.

JOYFUL PLAY

There are a lot of misconceptions floating around about people who write fan fiction and why they write it, so let's knock off a few of them right up front. Fan-fiction writers are not pornographers. (This perception is so pervasive that in order to avoid confusing their friends and colleagues, many of the people interviewed for this article declined to be identified by their real names.) There's plenty of sex in fan fiction, but it's only a small part of the picture. Fan-fiction writers aren't plagiarists who can't come up with their own ideas, and they're not all amateurs. Naomi Novik, whose *Temeraire* novels are best sellers and have been optioned by Peter Jackson, who directed the *Lord of the Rings* movies, writes fan fiction. "Fanfic writing isn't work, it's joyful play," she says. "The problem is that for most people, any kind of writing looks like work to them, so they get confused why anyone would want to write fanfic instead of original professional material, even though they don't have any problem understanding why someone would want to mess around on a guitar playing Simon & Garfunkel."

Fan-fiction writers aren't guys who live in their parents' basements. They aren't even all guys. If anything, anecdotal evidence suggests that most fan fiction is written by women. (They're also not all writers. They draw and paint and make videos and stage musicals. Darren Criss, a regular on *Glee*, made his mark in the fan production *A Very Potter Musical*, which is findable, and quite watchable, on YouTube.) It's also an intensely social, communal activity. Like punk rock, fan fiction is inherently inclusive, and people spend as much time hanging out talking to one another about it as they do reading and writing it. "I've been in fandom since early 2005, when I was getting ready to turn 12," says Kelli Joyce. "For me, starting so young, fanfic became my English teacher, my sex-ed class, my favorite hobby and the source of some of my dearest friends. It also provided me with a crash course in social justice and how to respect and celebrate diversity, both of characters and fic writers."

Diversity: the fan-fiction scene is hyperdiverse.

You'll find every race, nationality, ethnicity, language, religion, age and sexual orientation represented there, both as writers and as characters. For people who don't recognize themselves in the media they watch, it's a way of taking those media into their own hands and correcting the picture. "For me, fanfic is partially a political act," says "XT." "MGM is too cowardly to put a gay man in one of their multimillion-dollar blockbusters? And somehow want me to be content with the occasional subtext crumb from the table? Why should I?"

ALTERNITY AND BEYOND

There's no way to make a definitive taxonomy of fan fiction, which is huge and ever evolving and constantly the subject of heated internal debate, but if you wanted to make a quixotic stab at it, one place to start would be with canon. Canon, in the fannish sense, refers to the facts and laws of a given fictional universe as laid out by its creator: Harry Potter is a wizard, his parents are dead, and so on. Some fan fiction co-exists peaceably with canon and operates within its constraints. You wouldn't think that would leave a lot of room for creativity, but you would be wrong.

Fictional worlds, while they appear solid, are riddled with blank spots and unexposed surfaces. There's a moment toward the end of *Harry Potter and the Goblet of Fire* when Dumbledore suggests offhandedly that Sirius Black should "lie low at Lupin's" for a while, referring to Harry's former teacher Remus Lupin. What exactly did Sirius and Remus get up to there, chez Lupin, while they were lying low? How low did they lie? (Cough, slash, cough.) Rowling never says, but that one little gap has given rise to so much fan fiction that "lie low at Lupin's" has become a recognized trope of Harry Potter fan fiction, a sub-subgenre in its own right.

It's human nature to press at the boundaries of stories, to scrabble at the edges, to want to know what's going on just out of range of the camera. Fan fiction teems with prequels and sequels, missing scenes restored and plot holes patched. It retells canonical stories from new points of view—the reverse-angle instant replay. How did the events of *The Prisoner of Azkaban* look from Neville Longbottom's perspective? Moaning Myrtle's? Mrs. Norris's? "To say that a story stops after we close a book is absurd," says Maltese.

Top 10 Most Followed Potter Fan Projects

Harry Potter and the Nightmares of Futures Past
By S'TarKan

Harry Potter and the Methods of Rationality
By Less Wrong (Eliezer Yudkowsky)

Poison Pen
By GenkaiFan

Harry Crow
By robst

To Shape and Change
By Blueowl

Oh God Not Again!
By Sarah1281

Make a Wish
By Rorschach's Blot

Time to Put Your Galleons Where Your Mouth Is
By Tsume Yuki

Harry Potter: Junior Inquisitor
By sprinter1988

His Own Man
By Crunchysunrises

On FanFiction.net

SOMETHING OLD, SOMETHING NEW

The way we think of creativity is dominated by Romantic notions of individual genius and originality, and late-capitalist concepts of intellectual property, under which artists are businesspeople whose creations are the commodities they have for sale. But the pendulum is swinging back the other way. In 1966, the year *Star Trek* premiered, Jean Rhys published *Wide Sargasso Sea*, which retold the story of the mad wife from *Jane Eyre*, and Tom Stoppard staged *Rosencrantz and Guildenstern Are Dead*, which borrowed two bit players from *Hamlet*. Both works fused homage and critique as surely as *Spockanalia* did. In her 2005 novel *March*, Geraldine Brooks filched the absent father from Louisa May Alcott's *Little Women* and took him on a tour of Civil War battlefields. *March* won the Pulitzer Prize.

These works aren't fan fiction in any strict sense. They're written for profit, and they're adorned with the trappings of cultural prestige; true fan fiction has naught to do with either. But they come from the same place fan fiction does: that moment when a reader enters a world that was created by someone else and remakes that world in his or her own image. If authorship is no longer the exclusive domain of the gods, it's no longer the exclusive domain of authors either.

There may be hurt in that, but there's a great deal of comfort as well. A writer's characters are his or her children, but even children have to grow up eventually and do things their parents wouldn't approve of. "We don't own nonfictional people," Maltese says, "and at the end of the day, I don't think we can own fictional ones either."

A Tale of Two Hermiones

When a stage version of *Cursed Child* cast a black actor in the role of Hermione Granger, many fans said that's who they had always imagined

BY SARAH BEGLEY

WHEN CASTING WAS ANNOUNCED IN 2015 FOR the West End play version of *Harry Potter and the Cursed Child*, some fans were surprised that the character of Hermione Granger would be played by a black actress: the Swaziland-born, Olivier Award–winning Noma Dumezweni.

In typical J.K. Rowling fashion, the author quickly took to Twitter to rebuke fans who saw this as a departure from the books: "Canon: brown eyes, frizzy hair and very clever. White skin was never specified. Rowling loves black Hermione."

She later called critics of the casting decision "racist" and told a U.K. publication that "Hermione can be a black woman with my absolute blessing and enthusiasm" and that "Noma was chosen because she was the best actress for the job."

But the casting decision and Rowling's statements of support were, to many fans, not a surprise. For years, a community of readers have wondered whether Hermione Granger was indeed written as a black or multiracial character in the first place.

Bloggers have speculated about Hermione's race on sites from Black Girl Dangerous to Hello Giggles, often articulating the way they as women of color identified with the character—an outsider in Hogwarts—as children. In past months, other fans have debated the question on Reddit and Quora, pointing out not only details about Hermione's hair but also that she's never specifically described as white.

A Buzzfeed post celebrated fan art depicting Hermione as black; the post's author related that the racial slurs flung at her as a middle schooler reminded her of the characters who called Hermione a "mudblood." And in *Harry Potter and the Prisoner of Azkaban*, Hermione's skin is described as "very brown" after a vacation—hardly proof, but it seems to be the only time her skin is ever mentioned.

Some commentators, such as Stephen Bush of the *New Statesman*, note that they've thought of Hermione as black since first reading the books:

> *[I] always imagined her as black, partly because, when she wows her fellow pupils at the Yule Ball in* Goblet of Fire, *she straightens her hair, which was, almost without exception, how in my part of East London, everyone's older sister prepared for a night out.*
>
> *So I was horrified a year later when [Emma] Watson—exceptionally white, no frizzy hair, and without Granger's prominent teeth—was cast in the role. How could Hermione be white?*

Of course, the illustrations in the Potter books appear to present a white girl. The illustrator, Mary GrandPré, told TIME in a 2008 interview that she didn't deviate from the book's descriptions: "I have this obligation and sense of responsibility—and privilege—to stay true to the writing." The casting of Watson in the films made the assertion that Hermione was white even more official. Most readers also assumed Dumbledore was heterosexual until J.K. Rowling announced that he was gay.

WELL CAST Noma Dumezweni won a 2017 Olivier (Best Actress in a Supporting Role) for her Hermione.

The Dawn of *Beasts*

The Potter series may be over, but fans have years of stories ahead in a spinoff

BY STEPHANIE ZACHAREK

THE CLEAR ANTI-FASCIST SENTIMENT OF *FANtastic Beasts and Where to Find Them*, a picture that arrived in late November of 2016, just as the U.S. faced a seismic political shift, might have made it feel like the movie of the moment. But it's not really a movie for any particular moment. While this Harry Potter spinoff features some charming and occasionally dazzling special effects—and was adapted by J.K. Rowling herself, using her 2001 faux textbook of the same name as a jumping-off point—in the end it really is dragon food, a product conceived to deliver more, more, more of something that audiences are hungry for.

There's nothing inherently wrong with that. But the picture—directed by David Yates, who also gave us the last four Harry Potter films, terrific ones—feels both sprawling and crowded, as if it were trying to pack too much mythology into one cramped crawl space. *Fantastic Beasts* is a prequel, set years before Harry Potter was even a zigzag-lightning-scar-shaped gleam in his parents' eye: it's 1920s New York City, and Newt Scamander (Eddie Redmayne), a "magizoologist" with insider knowledge of all sorts of magical creatures, is just arriving from London. Stateside, it's a troubled and troubling time: the underground wizarding community is under threat, because a whirling black whatchamacallit has been forging a path of destruction through the New York streets. To protect their ranks, the wizards must take great care to hide their powers from the No-Majs (the American term for Muggles). It doesn't help that a fanatical group, led by Samantha Morton's demonically prim Mary Lou Barebone, is out to break the wizards' ranks. Also, dark wizard Gellert Grindelwald has gone missing—in case you happen to find that *Fantastic Beasts* doesn't have enough plot points for you to digest.

Into this mess steps Scamander, hoping to research some new magical beasts and protect some that have become endangered. He happens to carry a number of such creatures in his mystically bottomless suitcase (more on that later), though

MAN AND BEAST
Redmayne, with his feathered friend, is the star of the planned five-film franchise.

their misbehavior ends up landing him, and the new friends he makes, in a great deal of trouble. Those misadventures involve Jacob Kowalski (Dan Fogler), an earnest, friendly No-Maj and aspiring baker; Porpentina "Tina" Goldstein (Katherine Waterston), a Statute of Secrecy enforcer who misperceives what Scamander is up to and tries to turn him in to the wizarding officials; and Tina's sister, Queenie (Alison Sudol), a charming flapper girl who can read minds as efficiently as a voracious grade-school reader tearing her way through all seven Harry Potter books.

There's so much going on in *Fantastic Beasts* that after the first act, you almost can't be bothered to care what happens next. In the movie's world, there's a magical explanation for everything, which means story logic too often gets left by the wayside. (In the Harry Potter books, Rowling did a remarkable job of making magical logic seem consistent and believable, and the movie adaptations followed suit; that clarity has been lost here.) And even though the movie preaches tolerance, its ideas never quite jell. Still, Yates and Rowling are intent on working their charm on us, and some of it sticks: if Redmayne's performance is just too adorably mannered, Fogler and Sudol twirl through their roles like dance-floor champs—both have low-key, breezy allure. And the beasts? They're often pretty fantastic. A puffin-type creature with a penchant for petty theft, a sort-of rhino-hippo thing whose bumpy face glows as if lit from within, an elegant green twiglike being whose demeanor is shy though his actions are heroic: these are just some of the friends who take up space in Scamander's incredible suitcase, which opens up into its own vast polychrome world of wonder. Most affecting of all is a majestic, giant Thunderbird, with a noble brow and feathers brushed with gold. This CGI beauty is the real star of the show, though he doesn't speak a word. His magic needs no windy explanatory exposition, which is why it's easy to love him best.

Potterworld Family Tree

The families in the wizarding world are intricately connected. Here's an overview of the most important families in the original books and movies, plus their connections to characters from *Cursed Child* and *Fantastic Beasts*

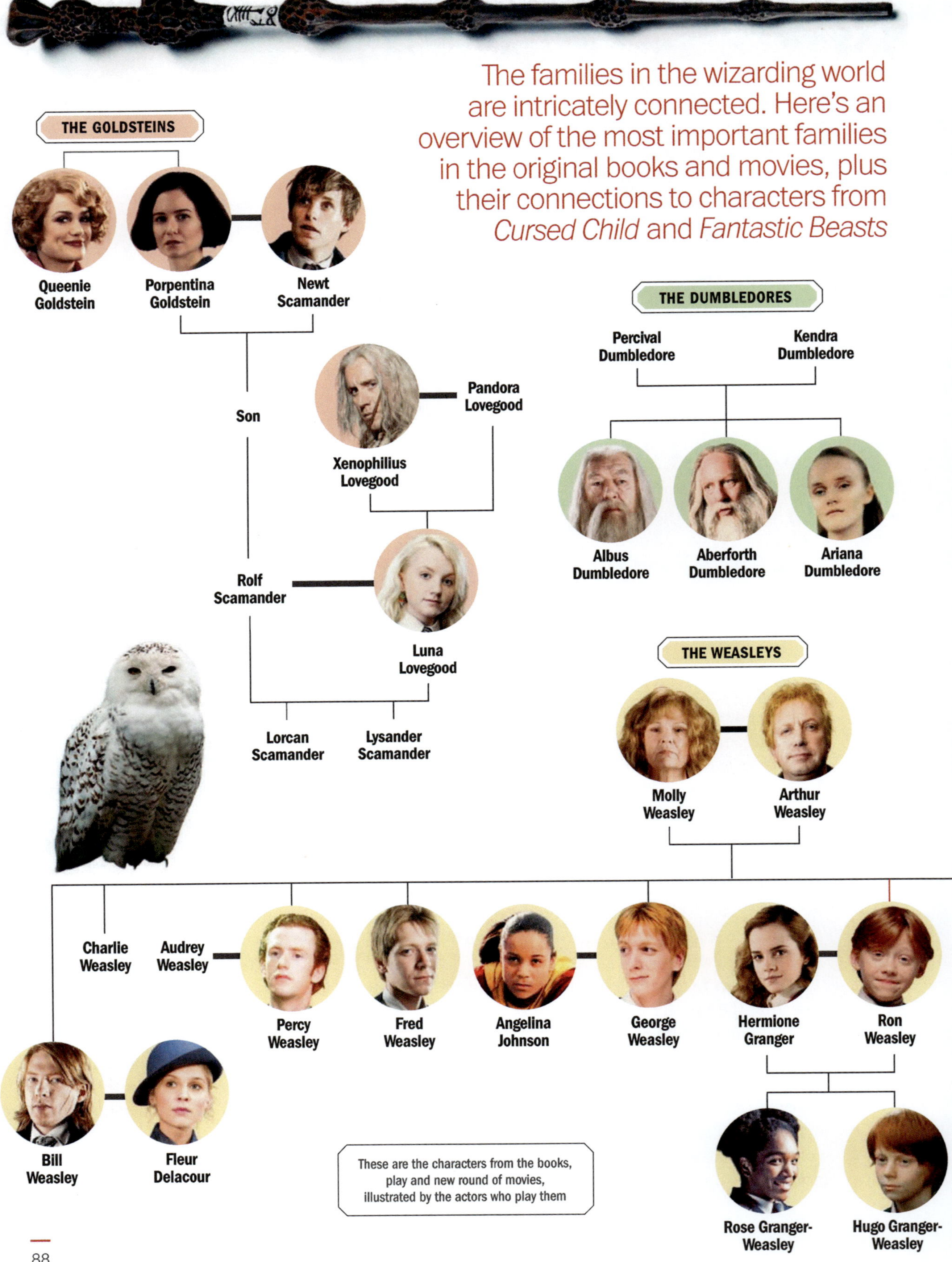

These are the characters from the books, play and new round of movies, illustrated by the actors who play them

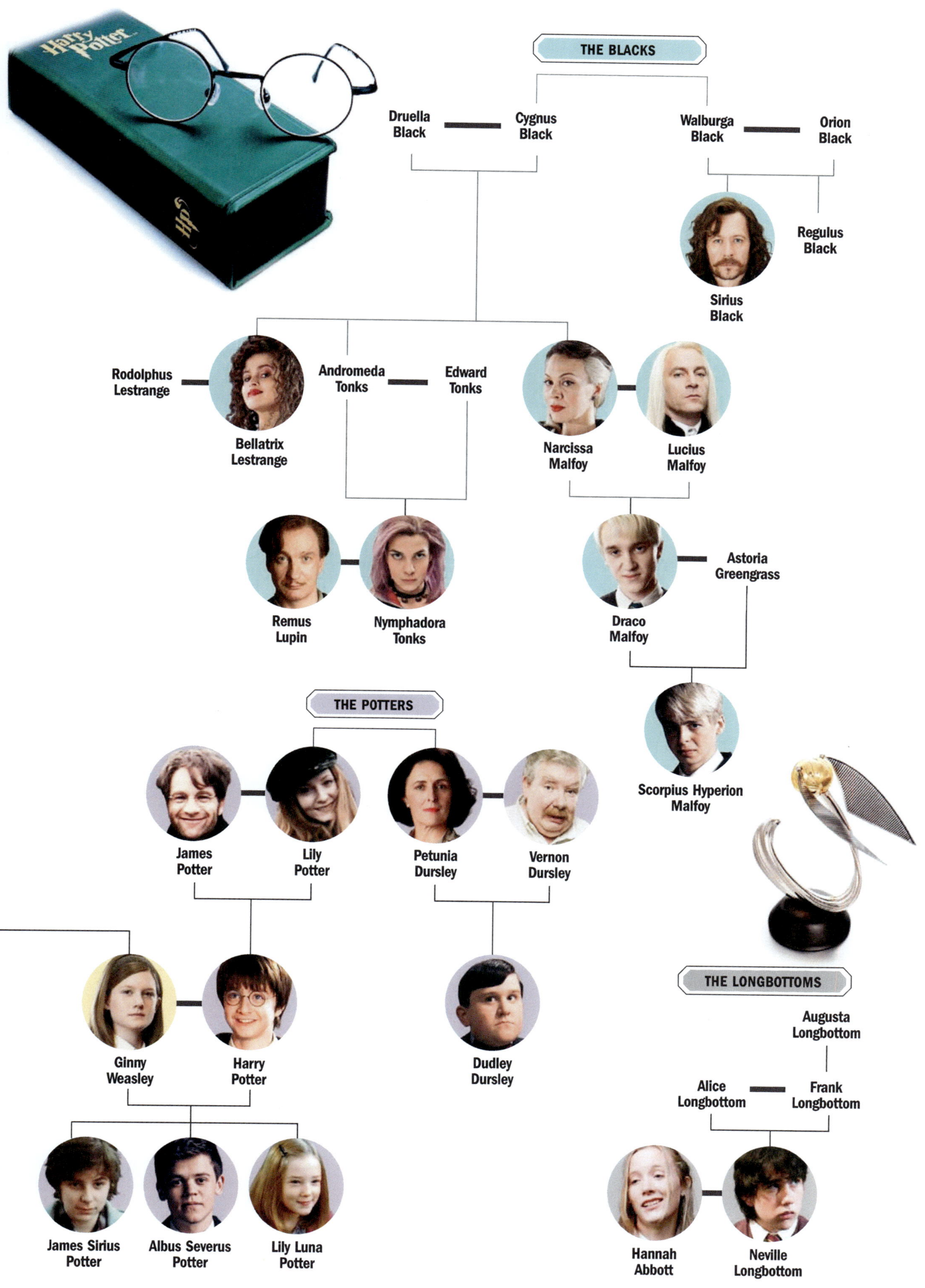
Harry Potter
HP
THE BLACKS
Druella Black
Cygnus Black
Walburga Black
Orion Black
Sirius Black
Regulus Black
Rodolphus Lestrange
Bellatrix Lestrange
Andromeda Tonks
Edward Tonks
Narcissa Malfoy
Lucius Malfoy
Remus Lupin
Nymphadora Tonks
Draco Malfoy
Astoria Greengrass
Scorpius Hyperion Malfoy
THE POTTERS
James Potter
Lily Potter
Petunia Dursley
Vernon Dursley
Ginny Weasley
Harry Potter
Dudley Dursley
James Sirius Potter
Albus Severus Potter
Lily Luna Potter
THE LONGBOTTOMS
Augusta Longbottom
Alice Longbottom
Frank Longbottom
Hannah Abbott
Neville Longbottom

20 Life Lessons from Rowling & Co.

Whether it's the power of imagination or the meaning of love, the author and her characters have plenty to teach us

BY ASHLEY ROSS

1. ON PERSISTENCE

From the very beginning, Rowling taught us to never give up. We learn this early on in *Sorcerer's Stone*, when Harry's letter from Hogwarts finds him even after he's forced to leave his home. No matter how far the Dursleys were willing to take him to escape this very important piece of mail, Hagrid made sure to get him his letter—and a birthday cake, of course.

2. ON POLITICS

Rowling, a longtime resident of Scotland, has never hidden her alliances, donating £1 million to the unionist "No" campaign prior to the Scottish independence referendum in 2014 and comparing some Scottish nationalists to Death Eaters, a reference to Voldemort's followers: "When people try to make this debate about the purity of your lineage, things start getting a little Death Eaterish for my taste."

3. ON THE POWER OF POSITIVE THINKING

"Happiness can be found, even in the darkest of times, if one only remembers to turn on the light," Dumbledore says in the *Goblet of Fire* movie. Rowling didn't write that line; it was added in the script by screenwriter Steve Kloves. Still, she invented the character who would say such a thing. And happy thoughts are consistently referenced as a source of power and light in the books. For example, a boggart, which can transform into one's worst fear, can be eradicated with laughter. And to successfully use a Patronus charm to fight a Dementor, one must channel his or her own happiest memories.

4. ON REGRET

Rowling has never actually said she regrets killing Fred Weasley, but she did apologize. And she does regret killing off Florean Fortescue, the owner of the Diagon Alley ice cream parlor. "I seemed to have him kidnapped and killed for no good reason," she wrote on Pottermore in 2014. "He is not the first wizard whom Voldemort murdered because he knew too much (or too little), but he is the only one I feel guilty about, because it was all my fault."

5. ON MEANING

Hagrid and Dumbledore may have gone by their surnames throughout the series, but their first names hold deep meaning. "The colours red and white are mentioned many times in old texts on alchemy," she wrote on Pottermore, explaining that some say these colors symbolize base metal and gold, representing "two different sides of human nature." These colors inspired the names of two relevant characters in the Potter universe: "Rubeus (red) Hagrid and Albus (white)

Dumbledore ... both hugely important to Harry, seem to me to represent two sides of the ideal father figure he seeks; the former is warm, practical and wild, the latter impressive, intellectual and somewhat detached."

6. ON PATIENCE

The wait between books felt like forever for fans. Most tried to wait patiently, but even rereading other books or getting costumes ready for the next midnight release party didn't dampen anticipation. Here's a breakdown of how much time lapsed between each book release in the U.S.

- Between *Sorcerer's Stone* and *Chamber of Secrets*: **274 days**
- Between *Chamber of Secrets* and *Prisoner of Azkaban*: **98 days**
- Between *Prisoner of Azkaban* and *Goblet of Fire*: **304 days**
- Between *Goblet of Fire* and *Order of the Phoenix*: **1,078 days**
- Between *Order of the Phoenix* and *Half-Blood Prince*: **756 days**
- Between *Half-Blood Prince* and *Deathly Hallows*: **735 days**

7. ON LIFE EVER AFTER

Through Pottermore, Rowling gave us an epilogue of sorts. Hermione Granger—who did not change her last name, like Ginny did—rose to be deputy head of the Department of Magical Law Enforcement. Ron Weasley, however, is balding and left the Ministry of Magic after only two years to co-manage Weasleys' Wizard Wheezes with his brother George. Percy Weasley, meanwhile, is head of the Department of Magical Transportation, while Neville Longbottom is now an herbology teacher at Hogwarts and is married to Hannah Abbott, a Hufflepuff. Luna Lovegood is also married, to Rolf Scamander (grandson of Newt Scamander of *Fantastic Beasts* fame). Teddy Lupin, son of the deceased Remus Lupin and Nymphadora Tonks, is now 16 and snogging Victoire, who is Bill Weasley and Fleur Delacour's daughter.

8. ON FIRST IMPRESSIONS

Just because people give off a vibe, that doesn't mean they're bad. Snape was always actually good. Mad-Eye Moody wasn't even Mad-Eye Moody! And do we even need to get started on Peter Pettigrew?

9. ON LOVE

From Hermione and Ron to Harry and Ginny, Fleur and Bill to Hagrid and Madame Maxime, love is everywhere in Potter. But not just romance. There's Harry's love for the parents he never met and the connection he has with his mother, whose love helped him survive Voldemort's curse. Rowling's most eloquent bard on the topic was Albus Dumbledore, below.

"You are protected, in short, by your ability to love!"
—*Half-Blood Prince*

"Do not pity the dead, Harry. Pity the living, and, above all, those who live without love."
—*Deathly Hallows*

"To have been loved so deeply, even though the person who loved us is gone, will give us some protection forever."
—*Sorcerer's Stone*

10. ON FALLING FOR THE WRONG PERSON

During Rowling's 12 Days of Christmas series on Pottermore in 2014, she spilled on Draco Malfoy, everyone's favorite Slytherin. "I have often had cause to remark on how unnerved I have been by the number of girls who fell for this particular fictional character (although I do not discount the appeal of Tom Felton, who plays Draco brilliantly in the films and, ironically, is about the nicest person you will ever meet)," Rowling wrote. "Draco has all the dark glamour of the anti-hero; girls are very apt to romanticise such people. All of this left me in the unenviable position of pouring cold common sense on ardent readers' daydreams, as I told them, rather severely, that Draco was not concealing a heart of gold under all that sneering."

11. ON NEVER GIVING UP HOPE

Rowling spoke of her own depression in a 2008 interview with the Associated Press, saying she had "suicidal thoughts." And in May 2015, when a fan tweeted her about potentially wanting to give up, she responded with a series of inspiring images and a message that resonated to many.

12. ON REVENGE

The despicable Dolores Umbridge came with some sickly sweet real-life inspiration. As Rowling revealed in a Pottermore story, Umbridge was based on a former teacher she despised.

13. ON STAYING IN CHARACTER

When Rowling had a new story to tell, she wanted to do it on her own terms but not necessarily with her own name. The author released the Cormoran Strike series under her pseudonym Robert Galbraith, and she impressed readers with the "debut" well before she was discovered. Rowling was unmasked via a series of tweets only 72 days after the book was published in the U.S. A group of forensic linguists examined the text to confirm that it was indeed by her. After the revelation, the book skyrocketed to the top spot on Amazon. Despite all the hoopla, Rowling still writes, and even tweets, under the pseudonym.

14. ON THE PRICE OF EDUCATION

In a July 2015 story, a journalist estimated that it would cost more than $43,000 a year to go to Hogwarts, including all the Diagon Alley necessities like wands, robes, books and so on. Rowling quickly shut down the idea on Twitter, clarifying that magical education is, in fact, free.

15. ON EQUALITY

Rowling surprised fans when she revealed that Dumbledore was gay, just three months after the final book in the series was released. The revelation is a powerful example of the message of openness that is woven throughout the series, and it's one Rowling has only continued to share.

When a fan asked about an LGBT club at Hogwarts, she confirmed that all sexual orientations are welcome, with a meme that read, "If Harry Potter taught us anything, it's that no one should live in a closet." She has been outspoken about LGBT rights and has called out "bigots" opposing them.

16. ON FAILURE

Pursuing your biggest idea can be the ultimate thing to relieve you from the stress of day-to-day life. "I stopped pretending to myself that I was anything other than what I was, and began to direct all my energy into finishing the only work that mattered to me. I was set free because my greatest fear had been realized," Rowling said in 2008, discussing her failures in her 20s. "And I was still alive, and I still had a daughter whom I adored, and I had an old typewriter and a big idea." In 2008 the author gave the commencement address at Harvard, citing her own failure as a key to who she became. "Failure gave me an inner security that I had never attained by passing examinations. Failure taught me things about myself that I could have learned no other way . . . I also found out that I had friends whose value was truly above the price of rubies."

17. ON THE INFINITY OF MAGIC

"No story wants to live unless someone wants to listen," Rowling told fans outside the movie premiere of *Deathly Hallows: Part 2* in 2011. Since the books came out, she's published three novels that take place outside the wizarding world: *The Casual Vacancy*, *The Cuckoo's Calling* and *The Silkworm*. But she's also used Pottermore to share even more stories from Hogwarts and beyond—and in 2016 she wrote the screenplay for Potter spinoff *Fantastic Beasts and Where to Find Them*. But this is Rowling we're talking about, so there's always more. *Harry Potter and the Cursed Child*, a play—but not a prequel—hit the London stage in 2016. "The stories we love best do live in us forever," Rowling also said in 2011.

18. ON OVERCOMING YOUR PAST

Draco Malfoy, who "was raised in an atmosphere of regret that the Dark Lord had not succeeded in taking command of the wizarding community," married Astoria Greengrass, who may have helped shape the bitter Slytherin into a better man. Rowling wrote on Pottermore that before meeting Harry on the Hogwarts Express, Draco, his family and other ex–Death Eaters thought Harry could be "another, and better, Voldemort." But "Astoria refused to raise their grandson Scorpius in the belief that Muggles were scum," making family gatherings "fraught with tension."

19. ON USING YOUR VOICE

Just like Hermione stood up for House Elves with the Society for Promotion of Elfish Welfare (S.P.E.W.), Rowling never fails to stand up for what she believes in. She often raises money for charitable organizations and uses Twitter to speak out about issues she cares about.

20. ON STANDING UP FOR OTHERS

"It takes a great deal of bravery to stand up to our enemies, but just as much to stand up to our friends," Dumbledore said in *Sorcerer's Stone*, when awarding Neville Longbottom points to Gryffindor for standing up to Harry, Hermione and Ron the night they sneak out of the common room. Of course, if he were around for Twitter, he'd probably say it takes bravery to stand up to Internet trolls. Rowling earned at least 10 points for firing back at a Twitter fan who had body-shamed tennis champion Serena Williams.

TIME

Editor Nancy Gibbs
Creative Director D.W. Pine
Director of Photography Kira Pollack

Harry Potter

Inside the Tale That Enchanted the World

Editor Claire Howorth
Designer Sharon Okamoto
Photo Editor Liz Ronk
Writer Sarah Begley
Contributors Jess Cagle, John Cloud, Richard Corliss, Alexandra Genova, Nancy Gibbs, Elizabeth Gleick, Paul Gray, Lev Grossman, Heather Jones, Megan McCluskey, Ashley Ross, Lily Rothman, J.K. Rowling, Andrea Sachs, Allie Townsend, Stephanie Zacharek
Reporter Elizabeth L. Bland
Editorial Production David Sloan

TIME INC. BOOKS
Publisher Margot Schupf
Vice President, Finance Cateryn Kiernan
Vice President, Marketing Jeremy Biloon
Executive Director, Marketing Services Carol Pittard
Director, Brand Marketing Jean Kennedy
Sales Director Christi Crowley
Associate Director, Finance Jill Earyes
Associate Director, Brand Marketing Bryan Christian
Assistant General Counsel Andrew Goldberg
Assistant Director, Production Susan Chodakiewicz
Senior Manager, Finance Ashley Petrasovic
Brand Manager Katherine Barnet
Prepress Manager Alex Voznesenskiy
Project Manager Hillary Leary

Editorial Director Kostya Kennedy
Creative Director Gary Stewart
Director of Photography Christina Lieberman
Editorial Operations Director Jamie Roth Major
Senior Editor Alyssa Smith
Manager, Editorial Operations Gina Scauzillo
Associate Art Director Allie Adams
Assistant Art Director Anne-Michelle Gallero
Copy Chief Rina Bander
Assistant Editor Courtney Mifsud

Special thanks: Don Armstrong, Kristina Jutzi, Seniqua Koger, Joseph McCombs, Kate Roncinske, Kristen Zwicker

Published by Time Books, an imprint of Time Inc. Books
225 Liberty Street · New York, NY 10281

We welcome your comments and suggestions about Time Books. Please write to us at: Time Books, Attention: Book Editors, P.O. Box 62310, Tampa, FL 33662-2310. If you would like to order any of our hardcover Collector's Edition books, please call us at 800-327-6388, Monday through Friday, 7 a.m.–9 p.m. Central Time.

Credits

FRONT COVER Greg Williams/AUGUST

BACK COVER (clockwise from top left) Jane Mingay/AP Photo; John Paul Henry/The Paducah Sun/AP Photo; Kirsty Wigglesworth/AP Photo; Lisa Maree Williams/Getty Images; Barcroft USA/Getty Images

TITLE John Phillips/UK Press via Getty Images

CONTENTS Warner Bros./courtesy of Everett Collection

INTRODUCTION Warner Bros./7831/Gamma-Rapho via Getty Images

TIMELINE (chronologically) Warner Bros./courtesy of Everett Collection; Urbano Delvalle/The LIFE Images Collection/Getty Images; Christie's/Getty Images; Dave Hogan/Getty Images; ™ and copyright © 20th Century Fox Film Corp. All rights reserved/Everett Collection; Warner Bros./courtesy of Everett Collection; Warner Bros./7831/Gamma-Rapho via Getty Images; Mikhail Metzel/AP Photo; Chris McGrath/Getty Images; Chris Young/AFP/Getty Images; Warner Bros./courtesy of Everett Collection; Pablo Paul/Alamy; Joe Kohen/WireImage/Getty Images; Warner Bros./courtesy of Everett Collection; Dave J. Hogan/Getty Images; Joel Ryan/AP Photo; Maurizio Gambarini/picture-alliance/dpa/AP Photo; Warner Bros./courtesy of Everett Collection

CHAPTER 1 **8–9** Hannibal Hanschke/Reuters/Alamy **10–11** Glynis Sweeny **13** Glynis Sweeny **14** Suzanne Mapes/AP Photo **15** Getty Images (5); AP Photo; Alamy; Scholastic **17** Amy Lombard **18–19** Universal Orlando Resort via Getty Images **20** Stephen Searle/Alamy **21** (from top) Chip Litherland; Joe Burbank/Orlando Sentinel/MCT via Getty Images

CHAPTER 2 **22–23** Mike Marsland/Wireimage/Getty Images **24** Rik Hamilton/Alamy **25** Gareth Davies/Getty Images **26** John Lawson/Getty Images **27** (from top) Kyodo via AP Images; Gabriel Bouys/AFP/Getty Images **29** Kirsty Wigglesworth/AP Photo **30–31** Warner Bros./courtesy of Everett Collection **33** Jordan Mansfield/Getty Images

CHAPTER 3 **34–35** Daniel Maurer/AP Photo **36** Scholastic (2) **37** Warner Bros./courtesy of Everett Collection **38** (from top) Warner Bros./courtesy of Everett Collection; Scholastic **39** (clockwise from top left) Scholastic (2); Warner Bros./courtesy of Everett Collection (2) **40** (from top) Warner Bros./courtesy of Everett Collection; Scholastic; Warner Bros./courtesy of Everett Collection **41** (from top) Warner Bros./courtesy of Everett Collection; Scholastic **42** (from top) Daniel Leal-Olivas/AFP/Getty Images; Cyrus McCrimmon/The Denver Post via Getty Images; Nestor Backman/picture-alliance/dpa/AP Images **43** James Keivom/NY Daily News Archive via Getty Images **44** Chris Rank/Bloomberg via Getty Images **45** (from top) Craig Stennett/Camera Press/Redux; James Keivom/NY Daily News Archive via Getty Images

CHAPTER 4 **46–47** Warner Bros./courtesy of PhotoFest **48–49** Charley Gallay/Getty Images **50–51** Mark Matcho **52** Justin Lane/EPA/REX/Shutterstock **53** Susan Watts/NY Daily News Archive via Getty Images **54** Press Association via AP Photo **55** Lefteris Pitarakis/AP Photo **56** (clockwise from top) Warner Bros./7831/Gamma-Rapho via Getty Images; Warner Bros./Collection Christophel/Alamy; Warner Bros./courtesy of Everett Collection **57** Warner Bros./courtesy of Everett Collection **58** (from top) Warner Bros./Entertainment Pictures/Alamy; Warner Bros./courtesy of Everett Collection **59** Warner Bros. Ent. All rights reserved/courtesy of Everett Collection (2)

CHAPTER 5 **60–61** Warner Bros./courtesy of Everett Collection **62–63** Matthias Clamer/Corbis Outline/Corbis via Getty Images **64** Warner Bros./courtesy of Everett Collection **65** Warner Bros./Photofest; Jaap Buitendijk/Warner Bros. Ent. All rights reserved/courtesy Everett Collection **66** Seth Wenig/AP Photo **67** Joel Ryan/AP Photo **68–69** Tannis Toohey/The Toronto Star/Zumapress.com **70** (from top) Jon Furniss/Wireimage/Getty Images; Philip Hollis/REX/Shutterstock; Joel Ryan/AP Photo **71** Pascal Le Segretain/Getty Images **72** Carlo Allegri/AP Photo **73** (clockwise from top left) Press Association via AP Photo (2); Chris Pizzello/AP Photo; Alan Weissman/Zumapress.com **75** Victoria Will/Reuters/Alamy

CHAPTER 6 **76–77** Warner Bros./Collection Christophel/Alamy **79** Warner Bros./courtesy of Everett Collection **80–81** Jamie Chung/Trunk Archive **85** Linda Nylind/eyevine/Redux **86–87** Warner Bros./Pictorial Press Ltd./Alamy **88** Andrew Twort/Alamy (wand); Matthew J. Lee/The Boston Globe via Getty Images (owl) **89** Courtesy Lenscrafters/Getty Images (glasses); Andrew Twort/Alamy (golden snitch) **91** Pablo Lobato **92** Warner Bros./courtesy of Everett Collection **93** Warner Bros./courtesy of Everett Collection **94** Rick Friedman/Corbis via Getty Images **95** Chris Dorney/Alamy **96** Warner Bros./7831/Gamma-Rapho via Getty Images

"Of course it is happening inside your head, Harry, but why on earth should that mean that it is not real?"

—ALBUS DUMBLEDORE

Printed in Poland
by Amazon Fulfillment
Poland Sp. z o.o., Wrocław